The Owl in the Tree

To my J!
Thanks for your
support on my first
book!. Hope you enjoy it!.
Love,
Peter

The Owl in the Tree

A Novel

Peter Kay

authorHOUSE®

AuthorHouse™
1663 Liberty Drive
Bloomington, IN 47403
www.authorhouse.com
Phone: 1-800-839-8640

Published by AuthorHouse   03/13/2012

ISBN: 978-1-4685-6430-3 (sc)
ISBN: 978-1-4685-6429-7 (e)

Prologue

Dear Mom,

It's been a little over two months since you left us. Each day is better, but the time passes, and the memories only get stronger. There are days when I can't believe that you are gone, and I wonder what was on your mind those last moments? I hope it wasn't anything that brought pain. I hope you were not scared.

My regret . . . not being there. Not being there to hold your hand, to caress your face, to help you move on to eternal life. A life I know you welcomed after the last few years. But God didn't want us there. He didn't want us to try and stop you. He wanted you home.

I have thoughts—thoughts that make me wonder how you really felt about me, thoughts that make me wonder if you had questions to ask, things to say. Or maybe you were okay. Maybe you didn't want to ask. Maybe you didn't want to know.

I do know one thing. I know that you loved me. I know that you enjoyed your time with me and that I tried very hard to make things perfect for you.

We all did.

I also think about the past. I think about what it was like for you with all of us, and with Dad stricken with stroke at such a young age. We were all so very young. It was so difficult for you, wasn't it?

But you pulled us through, and you took such great care of Dad from the day we heard he was ill. You never batted an eye as you figured out how it would be.

There I go . . . wearing my rose-colored glasses!

I think about the times we had and the things we did as we were growing up. I wonder if you ever felt that you took second place, second place behind Anna, Louie, Aunt Marie, and Uncle George and Aunt Anna. I wonder what you felt as I asked if I could go stay with them, at different times. Did you feel I abandoned you? Did you feel neglected? I hope not. I needed all of them at that time in my life. And I am so very glad that they were there!

It was just as hard for me to see Pop sitting in that chair day after day, not able to feed himself, go to the bathroom, walk, or even talk. I know we all felt something, something that each one of us dealt with in our own way.

I cry sometimes. I cry for all the reasons above. I cry for maybe not doing all that I should or could have. But I don't think you would want me to.

I knew on the day that Richard called to tell me you fell that time was running out. I knew that even though you did try, not very hard, but you did, that time was not going to stand still. I felt it every time I visited and held your hand. I felt the life leaving you little by little, and I could see it in your eyes.

The funny thing is, I saw peace in your eyes. I saw the eyes that were looking to see if Dad was there. Was he there waiting for you? I'm sure he was!

So now, I have written about us, me and you, the family. I want to share the good times, the bad, and the memories we had.

I want to offer guidance and healing help to those who may suffer through the same things that we all did.

I want to offer hope for peace and calmness in lives that are affected with things that we have no control over.

I share what we sometimes spoke about, what we sometimes laughed about, and what we sometimes cried about.

But most of all, I share the love that I have always felt for you and the fact that you were and always will be number 1! Always.

And so . . . here we go.

1

The Nursing Home

I WANTED TO start this a few years ago, when my mom first took a fall and headed for rehab. We thought it would be a short stay and an easy recovery as her hip was pushed back into place and therapy was the key.

Not so. The second or third day, as she lay on her bed, the doctor said to my sister, "This is going to be a long haul," and that it is—long, sad, and not easily accepted.

I can't do it! I'm tired . . . I don't feel good . . . I'll do it tomorrow. My side hurts . . . and on and on. No therapy. The rehab time was up. What do we do?

Prior to this accident, Mom lived on her own in a senior building. Not bad as far as they go, not the best place to be, but it was safe, clean, and easily accessed by all family members.

Even though there are five of us, none of us were able to have her live with us due to many issues. So even though she wasn't happy about it, she maintained a fairly good existence, had a lovely apartment overlooking the ocean, and had many friends in the building.

Good deal . . . for a while. When that door is shut and everyone is in for the night, it becomes quiet, lonely, and scary for an elderly person. But the sun shines the next day. Slowly the building comes to life. And all seems well. Then it gets dark. Oh boy!

Unfortunately, none of us are wealthy. Income for Mom is social security. Not enough to live on sometimes. Dad worked for the county—decent job, just not much money. But that's a different story.

We were able to contact Medicaid, and Mom was accepted and put on an assisted living program prior to the fall, worked out well for a bit—good care, carefully watched and monitored. Things settled for a time.

Today, a friend asked me if I were writing this because of guilt or to make me feel better.

I think it is a little of both, but I have gotten over the guilt thing. I do everything I can, so the real reason is to make me feel better and to hopefully make people understand how difficult this is.

Any thoughts on that?

So we were at the rehab center/nursing home. Nice place. Seems like they were nice people . . . NOT! Be careful. They may seem like kind, compassionate souls; but if you don't do what you came there to do, they would rather that you move on. We found that out and could actually see the change in each one of the caregivers as time went on. We were there from October to January. And if you think that Christmas was easy, dream on!

2

Christmas Eve

CHRISTMAS EVE WAS always a big deal for us. Every year, since I can remember, we had a big dinner. No matter how bad times were, we always had that dinner. And every year, it was the same questions, "How much fish should I order? How many pounds of spaghetti? Did we really make that much? That's too much fish!" Mom always made everything when we lived at home. After she sold the house, we had it at my sister's. We shared the duties, but Mom always fried the flounder! Always had to be Mazola oil and you had to put a saucer, upside down, on the platter for the grease to drip off! Well, it was always good, but we always had too much.

It's changed a bit now, not really the same anymore. But you know what? Change is good. It's good to start your own traditions. Do what works for you. Have the holiday as you see fit. But it was very hard that first year.

We didn't want to leave her that night, but we reluctantly did and went to my sister's and tried to enjoy. After a good cry, a little to eat, I headed home for the night. My brothers were going to be with her on Christmas Day. I needed to go home. I wanted to go home! In all my fifty-five years, I never left my mother alone on Christmas Eve, never woke up in my own home on Christmas Day until a few years ago! How did Santa know where I lived! Mom was kind of in and out of it, so it was okay. I was just happy

3

that the time passed quickly. This past year, I, my two brothers, and my brothers' children stayed with her. We brought food. My sister cooked some for us. I set up a table in her room, and we enjoyed the night. It was good, it was different, it was difficult, but we did it, and we all felt better for it! How could we leave her after all these years? How! I can't.

I'm kind of straying from where I want to be, but I wanted to give a little history and set the stage.

Now we're heading into January, and we have to find a new place. Rehab is over. It didn't work very well, and we can't stay at the current rehab/nursing home. What do we do?

We started to look and ask around, and yes, there are some places. The problem is that they only have so many places available for Medicaid patients. You know what happens then. They look for the most far away, funky facility that they can find. Some places are just awful. And you don't have much to say due to your status and income.

We all looked. My brother and sister-in-law went to some places to actually see them. Several "joints" were on the table, and none looked too promising. Time was running out, and we had to make a move. Mom wanted to go back to her apartment, but by this time, she hadn't walked in almost four months. She couldn't take care of her personal hygiene, had a hard time eating by herself; and due to macular degeneration, her eyesight wasn't good. Now with this disease, she will never go blind, but her vision will be impaired. It's like looking through a tunnel and only seeing what's around and not right in front. I will explain better later.

Fortunately, with some word of mouth and through some personal connections, we were able to find a place within a few miles of where we were—not a bad place, seemed to be clean, no horrid odors; two to a room, usually, one floor. But a nursing home is a nursing home! No matter what, it's still not a place you would want to spend the rest of your life in.

Well, the choice was made, the paperwork in place, and the transfer was on the move. I seem to have a little mental block here. I don't know if it was the reality of this, or maybe I just don't want to remember. But we did it. Mom was in place, and although not happy about it, all went well.

3

Rose-colored glasses

I NEED TO step back a bit and tell you about my younger brother. He is the baby in the family. There are five of us.

I remember as a child that I didn't even know my mom was having a baby, and she just came back one day with this little one. Funny.

I'm not going to go too deep into this right now, so I am going to jump into the older years.

I'm not really sure what happened in those years. I have always been accused of looking through rose-colored glasses at what's happening in the world. So what!

But I guess I didn't see things the way the rest of the group did. I didn't see behavior patterns or what was actually going on among all of us. I was more interested in having everyone over for Sunday dinner, having a party, or just staying home although in my younger years, I spent a lot of time with Aunt Marie. She was and will always be my favorite of my mom's sisters. It was a real tragedy that at the age of forty-eight, with four small children, she died of lung cancer. Was she a smoker? YES! First thing she did in the morning and last thing at night. It drained the life right out of me for years!

I'm straying again.

I'm just going to sum this up a little. I could go on forever, but I don't want to bore you. Let's just say that the relationship between my mother and brother was a bit strained over the years. For a time, we actually lost contact with them; and I think, even though they had a strange relationship, it took its toll on my mother. After all, he was her baby! So after a few missed holidays, birthdays, and such, they were back. Now they could be at each other again! No matter what happened, no matter what we did, what we said, it was very clear to all her family that you *never* talked about her kids! NEVER! No one was allowed to comment, no matter who you were. That's just the way it was from day one!

I can't even begin to tell you how wonderful he has been with Mom. I give so much credit to his wife for allowing this and don't think I will ever be able to give back to them what they have given to me. Yes, me, not just Mom. I spent so much of my life with worry, trying to do everything I could and sometimes being a disappointment to her, or maybe . . . to my eyes only. I don't think one of us will ever be that to her.

I want to step back a bit . . . well, way back.

4

First Avenue

WHEN MY MOM and dad were married, I remember my mom saying that the house they moved into was like her little dollhouse. It was all furnished, crisscross-patterned curtains on the windows, kind of "early American." She was very happy with it. Three bedrooms, one bath—imagine that! one bath!—living room, dining room, and kitchen, eat-in, of course. There was a nice front porch, a small yard and little room off the kitchen. It wasn't long before the first baby, my sister (who actually was a twin, but one died not long after birth), came, then my older brother, then me, then the next boy, and then the last. It filled up fast. We were in a real neighborhood, wonderful neighbors. I think my mother is the last of the women from that block. They were all great, and all of them looked after everyone's kids. They knew us all. It was a good loving home.

Actually, the entire block was a great loving place. Everyone on the block was an extended family. It was one big family and still referred to as that today. Unfortunately, all the major players have gone to their great reward, but there are still a few "kids" left.

It was definitely a street that became a part of your life, a place that was really called home with all the love and warmth you could imagine!

Across the street from us was our beloved Mrs. LaFrance. Wonderful sweet lady with a terrific family! Her daughter and grandchildren visited every summer. Aunt Gia was the best and always took us to the beach. Mrs. LaFrance had a difficult time reading English. She was Italian. She would have my older brother read the racing forms to her, and together they bet on the horses! That's why he's in love with them to this day!

The three granddaughters were the most fun! They were very close to us and especially to my sister. They enjoyed some wonderful times together as they grew up. But unfortunately, as with many, as you grow up, you grow apart. You forget, but you don't forget all those wonderful times during the hot summers of First Avenue!

Naturally, the house became too small for five kids and two parents. So off we went to a newer home with four bedrooms and one and one-half bath! Yeah!

From there, life fell off the mountain. I guess we were there for a few years when my father had a stroke. He was fifty-three. My mom was forty. Holy shit! Now what? Five kids, new house, mortgage, heating, electric, and food *and* school! Oh boy!

Thank you, God, for our grandparents, family, and friends. They got us through many tough times, and my sister was the oldest. I guess she became the "mom" as ours had some really tough days ahead of her. Dad wasn't supposed to make it through the week, how much more, guess what? seventeen years! Seventeen years she took care of him, and us. But as we are getting older, I hear things that I didn't know, things I didn't see, or maybe didn't want to. But we held together, we ate, we had a roof over our heads, and we had each other. Not in the sense of the basic TV family, but we always knew our backs were covered. No matter what. Even to this day. We may be apart, living in different towns—well, I am anyway—but we'll always be there.

There was a very short time that Dad was in the VA hospital, very short. My mom would leave work early, get a ride up there, and see how things were. They were awful. He wasn't cared for, and he was left alone, not able to feed himself or anything else. She couldn't take it. She brought him home. Home . . . where we all lived. Home to be with everyone so she could care for him. Who knew it would be seventeen years! It was tough, but we all did what we could. There's much more, but I think I better continue with the theme.

From that house, after we all kind of moved out, it was time to sell. Too many things needed to be done, and the upkeep was getting out of control.

A new senior building opened up, and Mom put the house up for sale, got a really nice one-bedroom apartment near the ocean (not the one she is in now), and we moved them there. *Wow!* Was that a hard day! When I left that first time, I cried all the way home as I felt like we abandoned them and it was very difficult to deal with. But it was good. She had more money to work with, no upkeep, new things in the apartment, and Dad was taken care of with some help from an aide.

Well, I can't remember how long they were there, not long before they discovered an aneurism. He was in the hospital at the time, but she wanted to bring him home. Not much they could do, he would probably just close his eyes and slip away comfortably. There is one thing I will never forget while we were with him in the hospital. We were there—me, my second-from-the-younger brother and Mom. I remember my dad. He took my mom's hand, took my brother's hand, and placed it over hers. He wanted to make sure he would watch over her. I'll never forget it. He came home. A week later, my youngest brother and I spent the weekend there. For some reason, his sister (ninety-three years old now) and others came to visit. He died that morning. I think it was a Sunday. Quietly, peacefully, after seventeen years! The paramedics wanted to revive him. Why? I don't know.

5

Sisters

Now Mom was on her own, and it was a big adjustment—no one to actually care for anymore, no worries about going out and hurrying back to take care of Dad. Was this a good thing? Yes and no. Yes, because she didn't have to worry; but no, because it was hard for her to adjust. She did take a little job cooking for the priests at the local parish. This was good for her. She got out, did what she could, drove the car to and from; and things settled out.

Then another large obstacle entered the scene. Her sister was also a widow and living alone. The other sister thought it would be a good idea for them to live together. But where? How? When?

They began looking around and decided to go to an apartment building that my aunt had been living in. Now what happens when you put two grown women in a one-bedroom apartment? You tell me.

There are conflicting stories on what exactly prompted the one-bedroom apartment. Some will not agree with me on what I saw and heard, but like I said, it's my story and what I remember.

The idea was to have them together, and after looking at many places, the decision was to go to the one-bedroom apartment. I will say that each one of us was asked how we felt about it. I believe that my older brother was the one who spoke up and thought it might not be a good idea with

11

one bedroom and bath. There were others available—two bedrooms, two baths in the building, but I seem to remember that the balcony was the selling point. I don't believe that either of them actually agreed together, but they did it, and we did what we could to help.

For almost fifteen years they lived together, fought together, lived together . . . did I say fought together? Sometimes it was just awful. My other aunt actually owned the apartment. She was very generous, and they only had to pay the maintenance fee as rent. Good deal, yes? Not really. It just went on and on until the day came when she had to leave.

You see, my mom was very vocal about how she felt, and you always knew where you stood with her. No bull, no games, she called it as she saw it! Many weren't impressed with that.

She always threatened that she would move out someday, and I guess it became too much for the sister that owned the place. One day, she called my sister and told her that my mom had to move out. That was it. It was in a fit of anger, maybe not meant the way it came out; but nevertheless, it was out, and we had to deal with it. I don't believe her sister that she lived with was happy with the decision, but we moved fast and did what we had to do. We always took care of Mom, and I would never stand for anyone hurting her in any way!

It was a sad day when we moved her, but it had to be done.

We were lucky once again with my brother working for the city and having other connections. We got her the apartment in a different senior building—really nice, seventh floor, wonderful view of the ocean. Fred and I bought her some new furniture and accessories, and all the kids chipped in to get the final payments and other things she needed. Nice.

For a while.

6

The Apartment

You know, it's funny. My mother always said that she wanted to move into this particular building, always threatened to do so, but never did it.

Now they did have some nice times when they lived together, and they were good company, but as I said in the previous chapter, we should have looked for a two-bedroom place. You just can't put two grown women into a one-bedroom apartment. You just can't.

Things settled down, and all was okay for a time. We bought all-new kitchen stuff, fixed up the bedroom nice, and wallpapered the bathroom, made it homier for her. I visited often, did what I could, made sure she did not want for anything. We all did.

Every Friday was hair day at the salon in the building, social hour. It seemed to be a good thing. She had several friends in the building, and they did many things together. Even had a ninety-something that still drove! How about that? I think she is still going at one hundred, but not driving. Thank God!

Then we had a bit of a setback. The doctors discovered an aneurysm, and this they could operate on. So we made the appointments. My sister took her for her doctor visits, and the operation was performed. It was in January. I remember that time well. Mom was just home from the hospital, and I received a call that my wonderful godmother had passed away. Oh boy, I could go on about them forever, but I will stay in line here. Anyway, I didn't tell her right away as it would be too much for her to hear at this moment. She was in her eighties, did have some physical issues; but as with any death, it's a shock and a sad time.

I made arrangements with my sister and brothers for Mom, and off I went to the funeral.

I told her about it a few days later when she was feeling better. What can I say! They shared so many good times in life. My mom, dad, uncle, and aunt. They were my godparents. Uncle George died many years before. How? Had a stroke too. But let me tell you something funny. He would insist to my aunt that he had to come visit my mom and dad. Now, my dad was sick with his stroke at the same time. They would come down, as they lived in New York, and the two men would carry on a conversation between each other, and neither one of them could complete a word, let alone a sentence. My mom and aunt would just shake their heads and chuckle, but they did communicate, and they did laugh their asses off sometimes. He only visited maybe once or twice. On his last visit, he didn't want to leave, but they did, and several weeks later he perished in a house fire. Terribly sad!

But thankfully, we all have so many fond memories. One of those is his midnight visits. He owned a restaurant, would close up at midnight, drive to Chinatown in NYC, load the trunk up with food, head to our house, get there around two or so in the morning, wake us all up, eat, and go back to sleep. Can't beat that, can you? God bless them both!

So after the operation, things got worse. More care was needed, and that's when we got the Medicaid initiated and the assisted living help. It went well for a while. As with everything, we would all share in the duties, arrange things so visits were often, and it wasn't easy.

7

The Family

I'D LIKE TO take a moment to give all my characters names. It will make it much easier to write this and to understand things.

Let's start from the oldest to the youngest:

We have Susan, Steve, and Peter (that's me!), Richard, and Michael.

Susan is married to Garrett. They have four children, one daughter-in-law, one son-in-law, and almost two grandchildren.

Steve is married to Diane. They live down the street from where my mom is.

Peter, that's me, has a partner Fred, and lives in Pennsylvania with two dogs and Erna, Fred's mom.

Richard, recently divorced from Tami, has three children.

Michael is married to Maryann, no children, one cat (more like a child though).

So here we are.

Now just in case you are wondering why Michael is there every day, let me tell you. He is on disability from the state, so he has the time to be with her.

Richard works close by, so he goes almost every day at lunch time.

Let's go back to the apartment and the operation.

It took a while for Mom to start feeling better, and we had to have someone in the evening to stay with her for a few nights. After that, between Susan and Maryann, she wasn't alone at night.

After a while, she started to walk, go out again, at least to get her hair done and an occasional lunch. We had the assisted living program started, and they were monitoring her daily. Her meds were put in order. They would come in and heat up her food if no one was there and help her to get dressed.

I would try to cook things for her on the weekends, and the rest of the group would bring food.

Richard did her shopping and kept her freezer and pantry full.

Everyone made sure there was always enough to eat.

It still was difficult. She really hated to be alone, never really felt happy about it, but there wasn't anything we could do. The building was secure, she was safe inside, and one of us was always close by.

She continued her daily routine, visited her friends, but I must say a bit less frequently. She didn't go to get her hair done every week and was going out less and less.

It was on a Saturday—she changed her hair day somewhere along the way—that she came back from getting her hair done, entered the apartment, got very dizzy (she was having dizzy spells and had medication for that), went to get her pills, and fell on the floor.

Fortunately, she had the life alert around her neck and was able to summon help. They were there within minutes and took her to the hospital.

We had a list on the door with all the phone numbers and who to call first, second, third, etc.

I was on my way to a wedding, and Fred was on a much-needed vacation in Florida that weekend. Richard called to tell me that Mom fell.

She was in the hospital, and they weren't sure if her hip was broken or not. He told me not to come yet. They would be in the emergency room for a long time. Susan and Michael were there. Susan has power of attorney for her.

Now I had to get someone to watch Erna so I could go down there the next day. Fortunately, I have great friends from work, and they stayed so I could go.

And now we start. Oh boy!

8

Rehab

WELL, IT WAS a long stay in the hospital, but they couldn't keep her any longer. We were able to get her into a rather new facility not far from her home. My mother was okay with this. She thought it was going to be a good place. You see, her sister had knee surgery and went here for therapy, did very well. That's the issue. One did well. One did not. Guess who didn't?

Mom was there from the end of October to January. We went through the holidays as I spoke of earlier. It was a difficult time for all of us. Thanksgiving is not a big deal. She was okay with not being a part of that. We all kind of do our own thing at that time.

It used to be, way back when, that we had Thanksgiving at home (when Mom had her home) and my dad's sister and family came for dinner. It was always a good time, lots of fun, and we all looked forward to it. Well, I think everyone did.

Then, we went to my sister's; and because of the number of people, my aunt and her family stopped coming. Sometimes we had as many as twenty-four people there! That's a lot for the turkey day!

The tradition was dinner on Thursday, and then I would decorate my sister's house on the outside for Christmas on Friday. Rain, snow, whatever, it was always on that day for years! After I had my own home, it was difficult for me, and I really felt it was time for me to start my own traditions. My sister's family took over, and they always do a great job! Of course, my decorating outside was superb! LOL!

We started to have our own Thanksgivings at home, and since my cousin Carol and John live close to me, Aunt Sophie and her family came to us. We are still doing it, but I don't know for how long. People are getting older, and the travel is getting a bit tough. But we'll see. It is a nice day. We do look forward to it. I remember, one year, we were real crazy here and invited twenty-five people for Thanksgiving dinner! We have a very large sunroom, and I cleared it out, rented tables and chairs and cooked like there was no tomorrow! *Too much work!* Stupidly, we tried it once more and finally had settled for ten to twelve. Plenty! It was a relaxing time.

Well, back to the home.

Since the painkillers were working, we kind of sailed through the holiday without too much trouble.

Now it was the end of December, and we had to find a new place quickly. They needed the bed, and there wasn't any room in the nursing facility for Mom. We had to move and move quick . . . in the dead of winter!

Before we leave there, let me tell you about Sara. Sara worked with the priests after my mom did the cooking for them. We went to school with her kids, and my brother and I worked with her son and daughter. Sara was a delightful woman—very vivacious, funny, and, I think, complaining all the time. But she was in the room across from my mom. We didn't know what was wrong in the beginning, but we knew that she was suffering from Alzheimer's. I know it's not nice to laugh, but she really did make us laugh! She loved coffee from Dunkin Donuts, and Richard would bring her a cup when he visited. If he didn't bring it, she would ask for it! How she remembered that! Every time we were there, we made sure we went to see her, and she was in a wheelchair and would come and join us for a visit. She knew my mom, but didn't always remember her. That's okay. One night, I took both ladies to the dining room for dinner. She was very happy, and we had as nice a time as we could. We found out shortly after that she had cancer. Nothing could be done; and thankfully, in her condition, for some God-given reason, she never said she was in any kind of pain. It was just amazing! She passed away not too long after we left there. I would consider that a good thing!

So after much research, visiting places and looking around, we were able to get Mom into a facility about a mile away. Not a bad place—I may have mentioned that before.

We moved her over by ambulance, settled her in, and hoped for the best.

Therapy was started again, same story—*too tired, don't feel good, stomach hurts, I can't do it!* Over and over and over . . . it was over. No more therapy.

Now, we still had her apartment. In the middle of all of this, the building was being renovated! They were starting on the top floors (there were twenty-eight floors there) and had to move the people out of their apartments into empty ones for six weeks. Right! It took longer than that. But anyway, we packed up her place, and right at that time, I knew she would never be back. We packed everything, cleaned out what needed to be cleaned, threw out what we could, and they moved her stuff to a different floor. We still hung on to the dream that she might come home and waited for the apartment to be finished.

In the meantime, the new apartment was on a higher floor with a great center view of the ocean and seemed a bit larger. We asked if she could stay there, and they said yes. We waited and waited . . . and waited.

We discussed what to do—we knew she would never be able to come back alone. You see, even with the assisted living, they wouldn't let her back if she couldn't take care of her personal stuff. She just can't. So we decided that we would have to give up the place. How sad. Beautiful place but they just wouldn't let it go on any longer.

Once again, we went through the things (never unpacked from the move), gave things away, and put the rest in storage. It really did break my heart, how hard it was. This may sound cruel, but it would have been easier if she had passed away. This was worse. We couldn't tell her because it would really upset her, so we danced around it for quite some time. To this day, I don't think she understands that the apartment is no longer. We brought her chair to her, which is one of those motorized recliners, a few pictures; and we hung some familiar curtains to try to make it better. We even brought over her TV set that my nephew bought her when she moved to the original apartment. Still, a nursing home is a nursing home.

Now we had the roommate situation. Oh boy, had some real doozies!

One lady was the mother of the head nurse there. Crazy as a bedbug! She used to kick my brother Richard. She would cry, she would laugh, and she would push herself all around the place. They finally took her out. For a while, Mom was alone. That wasn't really bad, made it easier for us to visit with a group . . . when a group used to go.

My brother Michael is there every day. Maryann is also a frequent visitor, and she actually was going to work there at one time. She knew everyone there and always helped out with either dinnertime or sometimes in the kitchen.

In the beginning, Mom used to go to the dining room in her wheelchair. Oh, I can't begin to tell you how heartbreaking that is to see these once-vibrant people not even able to feed themselves! You just can't know what it's like unless you were there.

We always included anyone who was around and tried so hard to make the best of it. A few times we had a family dinner there, but it was really hard. Finally, Mom said "No more, I will eat in my room." That's okay. It was easier for her anyway. It takes a lot to get her into a wheelchair, so she does better in her chair, in her room.

I am going to take a break now. Tomorrow I will tell you all about Ginger and Father Michael! Yes, Father (my brother) Michael!

9

"Can't I live with you?"

"Why am I here?"

"I want to go home."

"Is this a dream?"

And then the big one comes. "Why can't I live with you?"

Ahhhh . . .

"Mom, I have to work, travel, who will take care of you?"

"I'll just stay in my room. I won't bother anyone."

"But you need help, who will help you?"

And then even more . . .

"You have all those empty bedrooms and no room for me!"

That seems to be asked every time I visit. It's a hard question but unfortunately an easy answer. I still have to work, and Fred has his hands full with his mom. It just can't be done. No one else has the room or the ability to care for Mom the way she needs it. Michael has told her over and over, "If you get up, can walk, and take care of your personal things, we could make arrangements."

"Well, I can't."

At one point, when she first sold her house, Susan wanted her to add some space to her house for them. Dad was still alive then. She didn't want to do it. It's just a difficult thing.

Have you all heard the quote "One mother can take care of five kids, but five kids can't take care of one mother"? We get that all the time. Except now she thinks there are fourteen of us!

Listen, this home is very nice considering what's out there. She is very well taken care of and looked after every day.

Michael is there every day, sometimes twice a day for extended times. She really is in good hands.

So we have had several roommates. Some short-lived, one for a long time. Her name was Ginger, about ninety or so, and in a wheelchair. When she arrived there, from a picture we saw, she was in pretty good shape. Day by day, she became frailer—less time in the chair, more time in bed—and she had this penetrating scream! Yes, all the time, repeating the same thing over and over again!

We talked with her. She really liked Michael, and he would always talk with her, listen to her, if you could understand her. She needed more care, had to be fed, and couldn't eat anything solid. She had to have pureed food all the time. Looked like baby food or sometimes baby shit!

She knew his name, mine and Richard. She heard everything we said even though it seemed like she wasn't really there. Sad. I would sing to her sometimes. She would say "I like that song" or "I don't like that one!" Funny. Sometimes she would try to sing along.

She stayed with Mom for a long time. Even when they moved her room due to renovations, she came along. Her repeating and screaming was overwhelming at times. We asked to have her moved. They did move her out, but my mother said to bring her back. "She needs me," she would say. So they did. I think it was a good thing, although she did keep her awake sometimes at night. Ginger would sleep all day and then talk all night—the same thing over and over. Sometimes she would have to wait to be fed her dinner. Michael tried once, but due to her choking, he couldn't take the chance.

She eventually became so frail. I don't know how she stayed alive. The nurse said she had tremendous willpower.

One day Michael came in, and her head had fallen in her food. He lifted her head and gently washed her off. I cry at that thought, so gentle and kind he was to her.

Ginger passed away finally. I hope she is at peace and once again whole. How sad. Not much family, just a goofy old son who would come maybe once a month and sit there and ask her how she felt. I wanted to say "Are you nuts?" Oh well, God works in mysterious ways.

There was another little woman who used to walk and walk and walk all day around the building. Sometime cussing, just into the air! I guess she had some imaginary friends whom she didn't like!

They couldn't find her one day, looked all over for her. She was a tiny thing, and they found her asleep in one of the rooms under the covers! She's gone on to her great reward too!

Now Michael wears a wooden cross around his neck. Some of the patients thought he was a priest. Now whether right or wrong, he went along with it sometimes. One day, he told me that he gave communion! I said "What?"

"Yeah, I used a potato chip as the host."

Well, it is funny, but no harm was done. Some of them called him Father Michael.

Why not? It was a glimmer of hope. No one was hurt. It brought them a little peace.

There's a lovely Haitian woman who wanders around all day. She'll come into the room, just look at you for a bit, sometimes laugh, and sometimes just stare. Michael sings to her, and she responds to that with a song. I believe she speaks French, so we can't understand her, but she's happy. They have to keep an eye on her so she doesn't get lost!

Fortunately, you can't get out without being buzzed. Sometimes Michael talks with some, and they plan an escape route! He's a killer! But harmless! You have to make the best out of a sad situation.

I know it's killing all of us! This is the hardest time of our lives. Susan has a very hard time with this as she can't understand why Mom won't try to help herself, do things, try to walk, try anything. But she doesn't want to, and we just have to accept that and make her feel as good as we can when we can.

It seems that food is her only obsession right now. Even though the food there isn't the best, sometimes you would think that she was eating at the Palace Hotel. And between Richard and Michael, she gets anything she wants. She sometimes has two lunches! She'll say "I'm not hungry . . . what'd you bring?" Before you know it, it's all gone!

What else can you look forward to?

The other big issue is the clothes. You have to make sure everything is marked. They do the laundry there, so getting things mixed up is common.

One day, she saw a woman with her sweater on! "Hey, that's my sweater!" The nurse overheard and said she would get it back, no worries. Not much clothes to worry about, sweat suits, easy-fit stuff is all that works right now. Not that she was a clotheshorse, but she did dress nice when she went out and always wanted to look good. Mom wasn't into makeup and stuff, but always looked good.

As I said before, the hardest time of our lives! We are glad that she is able to see her first great-grandchild, and I think she will see the second due in December!

You know, you almost feel that your life is on hold, waiting to see what tomorrow will bring. Waiting to make your own life decisions and can't right now. Waiting for . . . you know.

10

Santa

CAN YOU BELIEVE this! It's eleven thirty at night in Kansas City. I have to go to sleep so I can get up early for work tomorrow. But as I was trying to fall asleep for the last ninety minutes, I thought of this lovely little story I would like to share with you.

When we were little—well, I was never really *little!*—but very young, we always believed in Santa Clause. I still do!

Anyway, on Christmas Eve, my mother used to work for my grandfather in his liquor store for the holidays as it was very busy. She would work until 10:00 p.m., and then she would come home and prepare a full dinner for her sisters and family for Christmas Eve! We were never invited! No, we were too stupid. We thought that if we didn't go to sleep at 6:00 p.m. on Christmas Eve, Santa wouldn't come! In bed, at six! Nuts!

So of course with all the noise, we would lie awake. My brother Steve shared the room with me, and it was at the top of the stairs, next to the bathroom. So every time someone went to the bathroom, they would stop by and wake us up and tease us that Santa was watching! Is that considered child abuse? I think so! Who the hell got us to do that? I still don't know. But they would have a great time downstairs as we anticipated his arrival. And I believe that the Christmas tree went up as well. They used to say

28

that we had arthritic trees! Probably because they were all a bit tipsy by that time!

I think now I would like to tell you a little about Mom from my memories.

We had a good childhood. Even though times were tough in the later years, we had a pretty good time. I have a nickname for her and always called her Rita-Bird! Don't know why, just a little fun.

She is a very good cook. That's for sure. When she was younger, she certainly hosted her share of parties and dinners for loads of folks! Mom was always able to make something out of nothing. I can remember when times were tough that she could turn a few pieces of chicken into a great pot of soup for all of us! She was also a master of party sandwiches. I don't remember too much, but I do remember that she used to make these party sandwiches for her girlfriends. They would get these large Pullman loaves of bread, and the baker would dye them different colors. They would spread them with tuna, chicken salad, or cream cheese and olives; roll them up; and cut them in pinwheels. Very nice! To garnish, she would cut thin strips of carrots, put them in cold water so they would curl, and add a toothpick of curled carrot to the sandwich. It always looked good! It tasted good too.

I remember she told us that when she was first married, she didn't know how to cook. Now my grandparents owned a restaurant. Those of you who might remember Jerry's Tavern on Kingsley Street in Asbury Park, it was an Italian restaurant. She was having her new in-laws over and wanted to impress them. I believe it was for Thanksgiving. So she borrowed the cook from the restaurant. He cooked the whole dinner, and then she served it. They were quite impressed and thought that my dad surely married into money! Good one!

We always had celebrations for communions, graduations, birthdays, and such. I remember those times. They were good. My godparents as I told you about earlier were always around when they were younger. Uncle George was a terrific cook! He could cook anything and make it taste great! He did the cooking, and my dad did the cleaning up. It was always a good time when they visited and always had plenty of good food!

Food—it seems like that was the number one priority. My grandmother would call, and the first question was "What's your mother cooking tonight?" These were the younger years. 1103 First Avenue, Asbury Park, New Jersey. That was our first home.

Many good times there—Easter, Christmas, you name it. Good memories.

We had some good times in the new house as well, but they didn't last that long as then my father became ill from a stroke. Things fell apart for a while, not an easy time for us and certainly not an easy time for Mom.

I know that my memories are probably different from anyone else, but these are mine. I have them and will always have them.

Mom was good to us, although she did have an Italian temper.

I can remember once when she became upset, probably over something one of us did, and the whole table of dishes ended up on the floor. My poor dad would say, "Calm down, Elizabeth" (that was her middle name), and he would clean things up. Her father had one of those tempers too. They all liked to throw things now and then. I guess it was common for the Italian temper to come out during an angry time. Oh well, nothing was ever thrown at us, except—

One time, when I was very little, we still lived on First Avenue. Mom was going to send me to some type of summer camp. Yuck! I hated the thought and didn't want to go. The only reason that I even thought about going was because my cousin Jimmy was going to go. So she bought me a pair of shorts, shirt, socks, and sneakers. *All white!* Imagine that! We had one of those old-fashioned refrigerators with the small freezer in the main area. Tiny thing. She bought us a milkshake from Carvel—chocolate, of course. We didn't have them right away so she put the lids on them and put them in the freezer. Because the freezer was so short, she had to lay them down. Well, being the inquisitive child that I was, I decided to see if they were really frozen. Now, a normal kid would have removed it from the freezer, stood it upright and looked inside, right? Not me, I opened it lying down! All hell broke loose as the chocolate shake cascaded down the front of my new white outfit! *Wow!* Since we didn't have a large house, there was nowhere to hide! Mom came into the kitchen to see what was going on, and you would think I put a knife through the heart of the pope! She grabbed my arm and one leg as I tried to run to the living room and get help from my sister and brother. My cousins were there too, and they ran outside and watched through the door as crazy Rita swung me around and around and finally landed me into the couch! Whew, I really did it that time! Wasn't hurt, just embarrassed as they all watched and laughed hysterically! Holy shit! Well, needless to say, I did go to camp, but it only lasted one day. Nope, never going back there again!

Sometimes if we really got her upset, she would take the youngest and say she was going to run away! She would leave us screaming and crying at the window as she took the little one and walked around the block. Too funny! We did get our share of "Wait until your father gets home!" Guess what? Sometimes we couldn't wait until he got home! He was the kindest and gentlest person in the world! I can't even remember if he ever got mad at us, let alone spank us. Rita-Bird took that department!

He was so kind. I remember when our dog Cha-Cha had to be put to sleep. In those days, they never told you what really happened, just that she had to go away. We all cried, and I remember that he came up to our room and lay on the bed until we fell asleep! He was a good man. I only wish he could have been here to enjoy his grandkids and to take care of his Elizabeth. She was in love with him, and every day now she says that she is ready to be with him. I tell her that he has a new girlfriend and he's not ready for her! She doesn't like that.

I wasn't the best of kids growing up, not a bad kid, just a bit difficult. I had to have things my way, and sometimes you would think I was an only child. I hated to go anywhere, hated to visit relatives, or go out to anything. I had to have a babysitter. My Aunt Marie! Her younger sisters married a bit later in life, so they had us to practice on! But I loved her so. She left us too young. That's for sure! She's the one that died at forty-eight of lung cancer. Now my other aunt, Lois, used to think I had dirty feet! She used to use Comet on them to clean me! How about that!

I have been accused of being the favorite of Mom, but let me tell you from my heart that she loves each and every one of us equally! Always had and always will, no matter what they say!

11

Anna & Louie

I'VE BEEN ASKED again why I am writing this. My answer—because I want to!

I want to write down what I remember, what I saw, what I think. I want to see it on paper—for me, for you, for anyone who would like to read it.

Who knows, maybe someday I won't remember. You never know.

I'm going to venture away a little bit. I know what this story is all about, where it is coming from. The thing I don't know is how it will end. So I want to share as much as I can with you, give it a full story, and then pull it all together when it does come to a finish—do we ever really finish?

My story here and now is going to be about Anna and Louie.

Anna and Louie, as I can remember, were friends of my grandparents and became very close to my folks and naturally to all of us. They didn't have any children, and I think my mom once told me that Anna had a miscarriage one time. But the important thing to know is that Anna and Louie were first cousins. Hey, true love comes in all forms!

Anna and Louie lived across the street from us on First Avenue. 1114 was their address. Most of the houses on the street were quite similar. They all had three bedrooms, one living room, one dining room, one kitchen, and one bath. Theirs was similar to ours, just reversed a bit. Maybe a little bit larger.

Anna was a tremendous housekeeper. I guess being Italian, having an Italian husband, and such was the way it was back then. She had a very clean home, shiny windows, perfectly pressed and bright curtains, and a great kitchen floor! It was a red-and-white checked asphalt tile. Anna used to clean it with Tide laundry detergent. Actually, she cleaned everything with that including her dishes!

She also used a corn broom to wash and scrub the floor with and then moped up the water. It was perfect!

Now Anna's parents had a working farm in Holmdel, New Jersey, about a forty-five-minute drive from Asbury. They spend almost every weekend there; and eventually, after Louie passed away, she moved there full-time.

Louie worked on the docks in Bayonne, New Jersey. I'm not really sure what he did, but I think I was told that he had an olive oil business. I think it may have been kind-of-Mafia type, but don't know for sure but do know that the family was very well-connected.

Louie really loved all of us very much. He was a kind and gentle man, so I thought.

Now remember, as I said way back, Mom tells me things that happened in her life, things we never knew; and whether it is correct or not, I am going to share that with you, shortly.

I always remember that when we were sent to the local store, Delito's, around the corner from the house, and if Louie was there, he would always pay for whatever we were buying. Always. No matter what.

I spent most of my time with Anna, so memories of Louie are sparse. I do remember that when I would drive with them to the farm, he would go over this small bridge on the way. He would say "Hold on to your birdie," as he sped up and went over the bridge! It was a feeling like you would get on a roller coaster! We would laugh each time!

Louie had a brother that lived in Italy. They hadn't seen each other in many, many years. On the day that his brother arrived to see him, Louie suffered a heart attack at work and passed away! He never got to see his brother.

I remember we went over to see Anna, and she was sitting in the living room, crying. I didn't know what was wrong, but his brother was there. He looked just like Louie. He took me in his arms and cried and cried! It was very sad.

After that, as if by magic, Anna was gone from the neighborhood. The house was sold, and she moved in with her parents and brother.

So now, we had to go there to visit; and of course, we did. I spent many weekends there, always wanted to be with my Anna.

When I was little, I used to call her NIA! That's all I could say. She always reminded me of that.

I was sick once with scarlet fever. (Was that possible?) I remember that Anna and Louie were coming over to see me. It was cold, snow and ice. My Anna fell and broke her leg on her way over! But Louie brought me a toy anyway.

Was Anna a good cook? You bet your sweet ass she was! Oh boy, if only I could cook them the way she could! Use a cookbook? Never. She could cook anything, anything, and it was always delicious! You can ask anyone who knew her. She was unbelievable!

She was too early for her time as Anna could have been a great TV cook!

I can still smell her meatballs, pork chops, and the best French fries in the world! Homemade! You just can't imagine what it was like!

Every Sunday was macaroni and meatballs! The best! Her table started out with just five, and before you knew it, there was as many as fifteen! She always knew that and cooked enough for everyone.

Now, this is funny. Anna always wrapped all her food for the refrigerator in tinfoil. Everything was covered in foil, even in the freezer! Nothing was marked, but she knew what was in every wrapped package! Never wrong! And nothing ever went out of the house without being in a bag! If she wanted to send a dish of something across the street, it went in a bag! Too funny!

The farm that her parents lived and worked on had a large packing house. They used to have tomatoes, peppers, squash, not sure what else.

They would grow them, pick, and pack for local stores.

It was a big deal. They would hire migrant workers for the summer, and they would live in this little house known as the summer kitchen. It was across the drive from the main house. It had a large kitchen, bath, and large front room. I can still remember the way the vegetables that were sometime stored in there smelled.

When I was really little, I remember that Anna used to put me in a bathing suit. They used to wash the tomatoes in large galvanized tubs. She would put me in the tub on a hot day, and I would wash the tomatoes! I don't think I peed in there. Ha!

It was a wonderful time, all great memories. Anna kept us going with food and money when we needed it. We would go for a visit, and she always gave each of us $2 when we left!

They also did all their own canning for the season, and that was a great thing to be able to have. Fresh tomatoes for gravy, pickled eggplant, caponata and . . . well, I can't remember all of it. I do the tomatoes sometimes. The first time I did it, Anna was still around, so she received many calls on how to get this right!

As with all things in life, it came to an end. Anna had this mark on her face. It was there as long as I can remember. She hardly ever went to a doctor. It grew one time, very large, turned out to be cancer. I remember going to the hospital to see her. She was close to eighty by then, never sick. She was losing her sight. I just held her hand, caressed her face, held on to her, loved her. She passed away a few days later.

I don't think I ever cried so hard in my life. Well, it was one of those times.

This is the juicy part!

One day, I was sitting with Mom, and she was talking about the days on First Avenue.

"You know," she said, "Louie wanted me."

"What?" I said.

"Yes, that son of a gun tried to get me one day. I saw he was on his way over, so I locked all the doors, and guess where I hid?"

"Where?" I asked.

She said, "In the attic!"

She also told me that Louie had an affair with someone.

"Who?" I asked.

"I can't tell you," she said.

"Yes, you can. He's dead, and so is Anna."

"Okay, Ida."

"*Ida!*" I screamed.

"Yes, and can you believe that Ida used to go over and have coffee with Anna almost every afternoon!"

Well, how about that?

You just never know.

12

Aunt Marie

I HAVEN'T HAD much time home over the past few weeks, so I haven't visited Mom in a while. She doesn't like that! But I do try to call often.

I have to wait until Michael is there so I know she will answer the phone. Sometimes the attendants don't put the phone next to her, and she can't get to it. But he calls me when he is there, and we chat.

Recently, she has been visiting her home on First Avenue. Well, in her mind. She still thinks it is hers sometimes. Today she told me that she went there and removed some of her items. She couldn't understand why the door was opened.

"Who did I sell it to?" she asked.

"I don't remember."

"Okay," she said.

That was that!

Tonight my friends, I want to tell you all about a very special person. It may be a long chapter, so get comfortable, maybe a nice cup of coffee, and I hope you will enjoy!

This story takes place, or I should say, starts in the mid-seventies. I was young, almost twenty or so.

I received a call from my dear Aunt Marie, and she asked if I could drive up and pick the kids up and take them to my other aunt in New Jersey.

You see, Aunt Marie moved to Dover Plains, New York, after living in Long Branch, New Jersey, from the time she was married—before that, Asbury Park with her parents, my grandparents.

Her husband, Uncle Dan, and his family owned a gravel business up there. On the property was this old, but beautiful, large farmhouse. Well, it was *old* and needed an awful lot of work. Aunt Marie said she would only move there if he made sure it was in perfect condition. That never happened, and she gave in, and off they all went! It didn't even have a decent kitchen, and there weren't any cabinets! It was really big, not well heated and needed so much work! *Ugh!*

But as they say, love is blind, and she did the best she could. I was there often, and it was a real trip sleeping there too—kind of scary, very dark deserted road, lots of spooky rooms too! I think the mice thought it was their private hotel! I used to worry so much about the kids, but they too adapted. She fixed it up the best she could at the time, even had an old wood-burning stove in the kitchen. I think she was happy, but really not sure.

I spent many of my younger years with her. She would pick me up after school, and I would stay there through dinner.

I was there for the birth of all four children, which included a set of twins. We always had a great time together, and she was so good to me—even before she was married, as I said earlier, they married a bit older than my mom and her sister Geraldine.

I would visit her at my grandparents, and we would do things together. We used to make these tree ornaments for Christmas. You would blow up a small oval balloon, get this type of one-half-inch-wide ribbon, and soak it in a solution. I think it was baking soda. We would then wrap the balloons in this ribbon, however we liked; and then when the ribbon dried, you would pop the balloon and have a tree ornament!

She also did this thing with artificial fruit. You would cut out a small circle, lay some cotton in the bottom, and add some small Christmas characters to the inside. Then you would add glitter to the outer edge, a ribbon for hanging, and there it was! I think I still had a few of these until we moved from the house.

She always took care of me when I needed a babysitter, and I guess I was a part of her life from a very early age.

Now her house in Long Branch was also large. It was actually a two-family one. After a few not-so-nice tenants, they turned it into a one-family. I don't know, but that was a spooky one too!

The bedrooms were upstairs, and you had to walk all the way from the back of the house downstairs to the front and then go up. There were two kitchens, one up and one down—breakfast up, lunch and dinner down. I don't know how she did it. My uncle was a do-it-yourselfer and liked to make things. He didn't always finish, but he liked to do everything himself—sand floors, build kitchen cabinets, fix oil burners, cars, you name it. He was an engineer as a trade, and the gravel business was his and his brother's.

So it wasn't always in the best of shape, but she kept it going, always fixing and doing to make it nice. It was hard for her; I am sure!

She was also a wonderful cook, and boy, could she make a mean pizza! She used to make the dough with potatoes in it, and it was terrific!

One of my fondest memories of her was when she would drive me home at night. We lived about twenty minutes away, not too far. We used to stop at 7-Eleven and have a hot chocolate together. Always, every time, it was like a tradition to us. Oh, how I enjoyed that moment. Hot chocolate, a wonderful person to talk with, and now a warm and tender memory for me to cherish!

Her other favorite was going to McDonald's for their coffee. She loved her coffee! She always went to McDonald's at 11:00 a.m. She said that was the best time for coffee, and the hamburgers were fresh! I think then they were about thirty cents!

She was so devoted to her children that nothing ever came before they did. She took them all over, whatever they needed for friends, school, whatever. She was always on the run. And I was there too! I am so thankful to have had that time together that I will never forget it!

Anthony was the first one. He was a great kid, but man, did he hate to have his hair washed! It was unbelievable what we had to go through to get that done. He would scream, kick, holler and go nuts! It would take me and Uncle Dan to hold him still so she could wash his hair. I believe that he is bald now.

Connie (Constance) was second. What a beautiful girl! She was born in December, so she came home in an oversized Christmas stocking. It was too funny!

Mary and Daniela were next. Twin girls, how fun was that! I remember when she was carrying them. She was so big! She would put things on her belly when she was watching TV, and they used to kick so hard and knock things off! They were summer babies. I enjoyed being with the four of them. We did so much together.

I guess you are wondering when I was at home? I guess it was an escape for me too. My dad was sick. There was always so much going on, but she gave me that little bit of peace for at least a few hours. Sometimes my mom wasn't happy about it, but she loved her sister, so she knew I was in good hands.

I think Aunt Marie was also born too early! Between her cooking, decorating, and other talents, she could have been Martha Stewart!

I really don't know how the kids liked going to New York to live. It was so far away, and it was so isolated. But they did seem okay when I would go there.

Earlier I told you about the call to go and pick them up. It was in June. I drove up and picked the girls up. I think Anthony stayed home. I think.

As we were driving out of the drive and on to the road, I glanced back at the house. Aunt Marie was sitting on the porch waving us off. I had this sinking feeling that this was the beginning of a very bad time! Little did I know, only three months later, she would be gone . . . gone—from me, from her husband, from her very little babies. Gone from a life she so enjoyed and cherished! Oh boy, it's still hard to believe that she is no longer here. Sometimes I dream about her, and everything is normal. The strange thing is I don't really know where she is, but I know she's home. I just can't get to her.

She went into the hospital a few days later for some tests, and they discovered that she had lung cancer. A smoker—I told you in another chapter that it was her one awful habit, even when she was pregnant.

They didn't really tell her how bad it was at first. We went to the hospital in New York, and she told us they cleaned it up. My uncle told us that they took a look and closed her up, and that was all they could do. It wasn't going to be long, but she didn't want to stay in the hospital. She went home. I would visit as often as possible. She was a trooper, didn't really complain in front of the kids; but sometimes at night, we would be alone, and she would tell me how much her body hurt. Her feet really hurt her during this process.

She did go for chemo. It just made it worse.

She was determined to go to my cousin's wedding at the end of September. By that time, her hair was gone, and she wore a wig. I remember that I fixed it for her before the wedding. She did go. She wanted to.

I drove back with them the next day. I was in the backseat behind her. I remember she fell asleep and her scarf fell off a bit. I choked back the tears and very gently put it back in place for her. Oh my.

I stayed for a few days and then had to go home and back to work. She went into the hospital in New York City shortly thereafter.

I made arrangements with my store manager to leave work at four every day, and I would drive to the city and visit with her.

Sometimes they were good visits, and others, they were just so damn hard! I spent as much time with her as I could and sometimes would just go out in the hall and cry my heart out. I went almost every day. We talked, sometimes sang a song as I held her hand. I only wish I could hold her hand now.

I was home the day she died. I was in the yard washing my car, and my mom called me in to tell me. My heart broke into a million pieces! I went to see my grandparents, and they were just sick over it. So sad . . . forty-eight short years with us.

They wanted to bring her to Jersey for the funeral, but my uncle said no. She would be there, and he bought her a crypt because she didn't want to go in the ground. I went up there that day, and I picked out her clothes for her viewing. My Aunt Charlotte came up to be there with the kids, and we proceeded with the funeral. Just unbelievable to this day!

I remember after the funeral, we went back to the "haunted house," and guess what was in the hallway?

Yup, new kitchen cabinets!

I visited for a while after she was gone, and it just seems that we drifted apart then. I don't know why. I can't explain it to this day. I hardly ever hear from the kids, all grown with families of their own. I don't know. It just happens. Does it? I miss them. We had fun. No regrets, none whatsoever.

My grandfather always called her the Fabulous Marie, and that she was. Still is in my heart.

13

Uncle George & Aunt Anna

"Hey, what's going on in there? What happened to this order?" Uncle George yelled as he broke through the swinging door into the kitchen.

"Nothing Why?" I asked.

"This last pizza that went out, the guy just called. It's missing a piece!" he exclaimed.

I stole a glance at John, the dishwasher, and then back to Uncle.

"Sorry, the pizza stuck to the oven, and when I cut it, I arranged it to look like a whole pie," I answered sheepishly.

"Well, now we owe him a new one! Let's not do that again!"

And out he went.

Was he mad? Not by a long shot! I don't think I ever saw him mad. Well, maybe once. Elisa may remember this if she is reading.

But before that, a little history of the two most wonderful, exciting, and loving people who have entered and, unfortunately, exited my life.

Anna and George, my godparents, lifetime members of the family, by some long, long roots—related somewhere along the line with my grandmother and her family and very good friends with everyone.

I remember some stories my mom told us growing up.

45

Aunt Mary was Annie's (I shall refer to her this way) mother. Very gracious from what I hear and very grand in style and life. My mom used to tell us that they would arrive at my grandmother's in a big black car driven by her son, Anthony. I knew him well too when I was younger.

Aunt Mary wore a big hat and was always dressed to the teeth!

So was my Annie! Perfect!

Anna and George lived in Elmsford, New York. They had two daughters, Dorothy and Elisa. Elisa came along later in life, and I believe that God had a reason for that. She was much needed in both her parents' life as time went on and they got older.

Dorothy is the strong one, very headstrong, very lovable, and very much fun as we were growing up. She took me to my first haunted house amusement ride, and we screamed all the way through!

George was an insurance salesman as I remember, and Annie worked in a publishing company for a while.

Then, as we all would like to do, George decided to open a restaurant. As I mentioned in a previous chapter, he was a great cook. The Emeril of his time! He wanted to open this, and he did.

I don't really know how Annie felt at that point; but I am sure, with the love they shared since schooldays, that she was ready to support him one hundred percent!

DeLisa's opened in Ossining, New York. I can't remember the year though, probably in the seventies as I was a young teenager.

It was named after the two girls, of course. I remember that my dad and some others went up there to help paint and get the place ready for opening. It was an Italian restaurant, offering a load of wonderful and delicious food!

The one thing I remember vividly was crab night, Tuesday night, all-you-can eat blue crabs. Guess how much? $2! Can you believe that!

We would go to the fish market in the city and pick up several bushels of crabs. I was scared to death of them, as was John, the dishwasher. He was a skinny black man who George befriended and gave a job.

We were both petrified of the damn things, and John would run like a nut if one got loose and ran around the kitchen!

"Yikes!" he would scream and run out the back door.

But he also used to scare me with them and try to chase me around with one if he was brave enough to hold it.

It was always a great success, and the fact that they were $2 was amazing. The money was actually made on all the beer that they would drink!

He would cook up all these frigging things, and we would listen to them as they scrambled to try to get out of the pot! Heavy lid, cans on top, and that was that!

Now even though this was a restaurant and he was a great cook, every night on the way home, which was usually around 2:00 a.m., we would stop at a diner and have something to eat! Yes, we did!

Now Annie was a waitress sometimes. That was a great time when we were all there—also, could be a crazy time if things weren't just right. Sometimes, and you would know, Annie was not in the mood. But once she went through the door into the dining room, all was okay. But back in the kitchen, oh boy, fireworks!

But we had a wonderful time, and I wouldn't have changed it for the world.

"I'm out of salt," said George.

"Run down the street and get a box."

"Okay," I said. And off I went. In this totally black neighborhood, dressed all in white, I would run down to the end of the road to this little store and get the salt or whatever was needed. I used to look like a white streak running down the street! But he knew everyone, and there was never an issue. It was a great place at that time.

One night, after we closed, we stayed on and had some dinner and then across the street for a few drinks (not me though, too young).

On the way home, as we're driving, Annie was a bit tipsy and funny.

At the end of the road was a lake or some body of water. She said, "George, whatever you do, don't put me in that fucking lake!" I remember that as if it were yesterday, and we laughed and laughed!

We had so many good times, and he loved all of us so much. He would do his night visits as I explained in an earlier chapter, and they were the best there was!

"You two talk more than you can shake a stick at!" He would say to me and Dorothy as we spent the whole night talking to each other. We shared the same room when I visited. Yes, sometimes the same bed. Got a problem with that? We were young, innocent, and loved our time together!

I spent many summers there. George and Annie were so upset when my dad got sick. They kind of adopted me, and I was there as often as I wanted to be. It was a second home even though it was far, but never too far. Whenever he came to visit, I would go back with him, and then he would take me home until I was able to drive. Then we would go up, usually me and Michael sometimes.

Then it happened. Uncle George had a stroke! Now what!

He was in rehab the first time I went to see him. I had just bought my new car and wanted him and Annie to see it. I was a bit apprehensive to go there. I was afraid that he wouldn't know me. But he did. He saw me. I went to him in the bed, and he held me so tight and cried and cried! We all did. Oh my, another broken heart for me. After a while, we took him out to see the car. I visited him often there. I recall it was the Burke Rehab

Center in West Chester. From there, he went home. I shared about his visits to us in a different chapter.

Prior to this and a few years before, many I think, my dear Annie was diagnosed with breast cancer. I went to see her in the hospital. She did have to have a breast removed. She was lucky, I guess, in the sense that she lived a good thirty years after that!

It was time for Dorothy to marry Paul. They worked together, and they decided to get married. Not sure how long they dated, not sure if she really wanted to marry him, but it went forward!

Wow! What a time! First, there was an engagement party of all parties! George even had a hot dog cart in the lobby! It was almost like a wedding!

The wedding was beautiful. Huge! I remember I was an usher. Had to get a tux and all. What fun!

"Dad," said Dorothy at the start of the procession, "I don't want to get married!"

She got married. There was so much prep work in the house for this. It was unbelievable! Cleaning, polishing, new draperies, carpets, the whole nine yards! After the reception, there were steak and eggs back at the house. I think it went on for three days.

Well, not the marriage though, it didn't last too long. Over and done.

We were back again! Just me and D.

Until Carl. Good guy. Nice wedding in the yard and reception at Gaulins. Honeymoon and the start of life! Going on thirty-odd years so far! Vow renewal at thirty years! And here comes Carl George, the new baby! How great! The love of Annie's life. George is already tragically gone by now.

Jealous? Somewhat, but this was her flesh and blood; and believe me, he was very lucky to have her as a grandmother. And she cherished him every moment. That was her little man, and she loved every inch of him!

Well, as it seems with everything in life, it marches on. Our contact was limited to an occasional visit and phone calls. My one call, every birthday, was something I always looked forward to. Always happened, no matter what. Even when she wasn't feeling good, I always got the call. I loved her so . . . always will.

The day of Dorothy's wedding, I remember I was in the living room. I looked up at the top of the stairs as she was getting ready to come down. She took my breath away! Beautiful! A stunning pink gown, matching long coat trimmed in white marabou feathers. Her hair was piled high on her head, everything in place, and her makeup perfect! She was a beauty! That image is burned into my memory bank.

She used to tell me that when I was a baby, she would change me and always give me a kiss on my birdie. How funny!

Isn't it amazing that both influential women were named Annie?

My only regret is that I didn't pay enough attention to George in the kitchen and maybe go to chef school. I think he wanted that, but a piece of me died the day Uncle George did and a bigger piece when Annie left us. My mother was just operated on, and that's when I received the word. Funny thing is she had Dorothy call the night before to see how my mom did. They were still close. Nothing could take that away. There were lots of jealousy in the family between my mom's sisters and Anna and George. Stupid stuff that created issues, but never with my mom and dad! They were like Lucy, Ricky, Fred, and Ethel. To this day, my mom tells me how much she loved them both and always remembers all the good times, like the time they were with us for Thanksgiving and the Turkey was so big it took the two of them to put it in the oven! They named him Tom. And the time Uncle George had a pork loin so long that it wouldn't fit in the oven unless you curled it up! Food, fun, good times, memories—that's what they made together!

It's unfortunate, but there just isn't that kind of relationship around these days. Is there? It was just so uncomplicated and loving. There I go, wearing those rose-colored glasses again!

Tough shit! It's my story, my memories. I hope you are enjoying them.

14

First day of school

"I don't wanna go!" I cried.

"You have to go!" said my mother.

"No, no, no, please . . . please . . . no!" I screamed.

"It will be fine, now get ready!" Mom replied.

"Mom, I don't want to go to school!" I cried again.

"Yes, your brother and sister are there, it will be fun!" said Mom.

My first day at school, kindergarten—I hated it and didn't want to go.

I continued my crying and screaming as Mom took me to school. We lived around the block from Bradley School, and I had no choice. No bus, no ride, just that long, agonizing, screaming, crying . . . walk to the death camp!

They took me up to the class as I was still hollering and carrying on! They told my mom to leave and that I would settle down.

No! I didn't! It was even worse when she left. All those little monsters looking at me like I was a nut! Well, I guess I was.

They tried everything, and it didn't work! So as a last resort, they took me to see where my sister and brother were. Not a good idea! I could see them through the glass door into the classroom. Susan was horrified at all the noise!

It sounded like an herd of elephants, made by one frightened little boy.

I wanted to go home, wanted to get the hell out of there! No. Not going to happen.

Let me jump into third grade a second. We were asked to write a story about kindergarten. I wrote about how I acted and all, and I used that exact phrase "It sounded like an herd of elephants made by one little boy." Guess what? The frigging' teacher said that was the most ridiculous thing she ever heard of.

"What a silly statement!" she exclaimed. "Whoever heard that a little boy can make as much noise as an herd of elephants?"

Bitch!

Probably ruined my writing career!

Well, I made it through, and each day was a little bit better than the next. I was a loner though, not many friends, none that I can remember from kindergarten. I did the best I could to make the time go as fast as possible.

"I don't feel good today," I would tell my mom.

"Unless you have a 105 temperature, get to school!" she hollered.

Never could we stay home. Never!

I think first grade was better. I enjoyed the fact that we could go to Fisher's Department store and get a few new things and some pencils and supplies. Not too much, just enough to get by.

By second grade, I knew I was in for the long haul! Twelve years of this crap and I had to go, no matter what! I tried everything under the sun to get out, but no good. *Get to school!*

Third grade was better. I had a friend from the neighborhood that went too. Lenora was a neighbor that lived a few houses down. Her dad was a fireman, and her mom stayed at home.

Nice folks, her mom reminded me of Lucille Ball—very funny, red hair, and she loved to sing and dance to "Calendar Girl" by Neil Sedaka! How do I remember this? Well, one day in class, I sat behind Lenora. She was picking her nose, and she flicked the bogger off her hand! Guess what? The thing landed right on my desk!

"Lenora!" I shouted. "Get that thing off my desk!"

She turned and was mortified and wiped it away. I guess that wasn't as bad as the day I had an accident. Yes, I crapped my pants, right in class! I can't believe it to this day!

"Get in the cloakroom!" the teacher cried.

I had to go home, had to get cleaned up, but *I got to go home!* And no, I did not crap myself every day!

I was kind of tall for my age, and this did not sit well with the rest of the kids.

"Teacher, we can't see over Peter's head!" they said.

So I had to move to the back. Problem was I couldn't see the board very well, so to add insult to injury, I had to get *glasses*! In the fourth grade!

Tortoiseshell frames. What a nerd. Now I don't need them, and they are the rage!

I really did hate school, and then we had to move, and I had to start all over again in a new one! How awful is that?

The kids in the new school were not friendly at all, and I had even less friends than I did in the old one. But I continued as once again I had to.

I remember when I was in third grade, I think. It was the year Kennedy was shot. There was a book fair at school. I didn't get much money from Mom for this, but I always had a backup. I went across the street to Anna and Louie on my way to school, and they loaded me up!

"Bring the books you buy with this here, and I will keep them for you," she said. How about that! So I hid them there. But on that day, the Kennedy thing happened, and we had to go home from school. I didn't know at the time why we had to leave, thought maybe I was busted!

But when I got home, Mom was crying and said that the president had been shot! Not a good day.

So I continued my way through grammar school. I didn't really have nice teachers and even worse in high school! They were so mean in those days, and it wasn't even a Catholic school!

I hated high school even more and not many friends at all. I did have a few buddies that I hung around with, but nothing to write home about. I wasn't very friendly I guess. I think I was just shy! You wouldn't know it now!

I tried to get involved in things, but I just wasn't interested, or just felt that I wasn't good enough. And the worst part of school—*gym* class. Shit on that! Climb a rope? Forget it! Basketball? Sucked. Football? Yeah, right! Then they had this stupid idea that we should wrestle! What the hell for?

My wrestling partner had some kind of scaly skin condition, and I thought I would throw up as I tried to touch him in the activity! It was awful! I can still feel that awful skin!

The really . . . really . . . bad part? *Showers!* I hated that. Why? I showered at home, and I will shower there again! No, no, no—only once did I succumb to that nonsense!

High school was a bust, and I guess I really didn't try hard enough, but I did make it through, by the skin of my teeth.

I didn't put too much effort into going to college as we didn't have any money, and in those days, it was very hard to get help. Mom wasn't sure how to go about it. I guess she felt I really wasn't interested. Dad was sick by then, so I went to work instead!

I got to go to work in the department store in our town. My mom used to take me there when I was younger to keep me quiet for a few hours.

The one store that I loved was Sears! I could spend hours going through the appliance department and looking inside all the new refrigerators, ovens, wash machines. Nuts, huh?

I still love them to this day.

I loved to go to Steinbach's Department store and look at all the display windows. I especially loved the Christmas ones. That's where I started some thirty-odd years ago!

Do I regret not going to school? Yes, I do . . . a little. I would have loved to have studied to be an architect and am sorry I did not go through with it.

But life is good, and I haven't done so bad.

15

A visit to Mom

I HAD THE opportunity to visit with Mom today. It has been a few weeks since I was there. She thinks it was a few years!

She was still in bed when I arrived, and I thought she didn't look too good. She was really in a deep sleep, and I thought her breathing was a bit labored.

I tried to wake her, but she just mumbled something and went back to sleep. I figured something was up so I sent a text to Richard.

"Were you here today?" I sent.

"On my way there in a few," he wrote back.

"Okay," I responded.

When he arrived, he was not happy either and decided to ask the nurse. I didn't at first because this particular one is a pain in the ass. She's always tired and has a sarcastic tone sometimes. He said he didn't give a crap and went to ask.

"Oh, we had to give her a sleeping pill," she said.

"Why?" I asked.

"She didn't sleep all night," she told us.

I and Rich sat and talked for a bit, and then he tried to wake her up.

"Mom?" Richard shook her foot.

"Ohhh," she said as she looked around.

"Look who's here," Richard said to her.

"Who?" she asked.

"It's Peter."

"Oh . . . how nice. I'm happy when my boys are here," she said in a sleepy voice.

She was awake, and Rich brought her an iced coffee drink from McDonald's minus the cream. I brought her a slice of lemon pound cake.

"I don't like that kind of cake," she said.

Rich said to put it in front of her and see what happens.

Sure enough, she reached for it, and life was good!

We chatted for a bit and were enjoying the afternoon.

The place was very busy, very clean, and smelled nice and fresh. It was nice to see how many folks were bustling about to keep things sparkling!

I encountered many familiar faces and was glad to see that they were still alive and kicking.

There are two women there that I refer to as Bette Davis and Joan Crawford. I believe they are sisters, but not totally sure. The larger one, maybe older, sits in the wheelchair, Joan. The smaller one, Bette, pushes her around. They like to play cards, and she carries around a video poker game. She always asks Richard if he wants to play. They don't have a great reputation, but they are always together!

Mom dozes off again, wakes, and then goes back again. *She really needs her hair done, but I will brush it when she wakes up.*

Before Richard came, I was just sitting there writing some things down. One of the residents stopped by the room.

"How is your mother?" she asked.

"She's sleeping right now, but doing okay," I told her.

"Does she like it here?" she asked me.

I said, "Does anyone like it here?"

"You're right," she said. "She's just lucky to have all of you to visit and look after her."

She then wheeled herself away.

She's lonely, a bit depressed, and when we first got there, she used to walk around in her walker. Now she is in a wheelchair, and that makes her even more depressed. She is very fond of Michael and Maryann, and they always make the time to sit and talk with her.

Another one was being pushed around by a young aide.

"Where are you taking me?" she asked.

"Just for a stroll around the building," the young girl responded.

"I am so damn confused! Take me back to my room!" she hollered.

Mom's up again, and we are talking back and forth. She insists that she was awake last night because my sister's grandson was there and she had to make sure he didn't fall. She said that she stayed awake all night looking after him.

They had been there visiting her the day before, so I guess it was on her mind. She was really talking crazy, and when that happens, we know what's next. It's usually the start of a urinary infection so they are doing a test today to see what's up. You can always tell when she starts talking a bit crazy.

Richard was telling me about her roommate. A nice lady, very quiet.

"How old are you?" Rich politely asked.

"Forty," she responded.

"Forty?" said my mom.

"Am I older than her?" said Mom.

"How many kids do you have?" Rich asked, just to make conversation.

"Three, but they only visit from two to three in the morning," she told him.

59

She moved a little closer to the windows.

"I think one of them is outside now!" she said, "or it's one of hers" as she pointed to my mom.

"What color are they?" Mom asked her.

"Black," she said.

"Well, they ain't mine!" Mom said.

I guess not! Not too crazy, huh?

I saw from the security mirror that we were getting company. In comes Aunt Lois and her girlfriend Carol.

"Hi, Rita," said Carol as she came and gave her a kiss. "Do you know who I am?"

"Hi, yeah, you're Carol."

"And who am I?" Lois asked.

"The pain in the ass!" Rita exclaimed.

Lois just laughed and asked if she could give her a kiss hello.

"Okay," replied Mom.

They sat and chatted for a bit, forty-five minutes to be exact.

"Okay, Carol and Lois," said Mom, "you can go now."

"Okay, we have our marching papers!" And off they went.

Richard was gone already, and we were waiting for Michael.

In the meantime, she was feeling very uncomfortable, and I thought she needed to be changed—kind of a strange thing to say about your mom.

Needs to be changed. Sad.

Marcy, the aide, came in and took care of her. We are grateful to all of them for the care they provide. I also need to mention that the ones that are closest to Mom are very well taken care of by Michael. Food, dinners, money, gifts, etc., are always given out so they pay enough attention to her. I guess it's okay to do that. You just can't leave them alone. Sometimes he gets there late; and the blinds are open, the air is off, and the room is stifling! They just don't always pay enough attention to just one person. But overall, it's okay.

I took a walk around as she was getting changed—a sad sight to see.

"Can I have an ice cream?"

"Are you having a good day?"

"I'm lost!"

Lost, a very powerful word in this place.

But the girls here are very caring, nice to the residents, and take decent care of them. There doesn't seem to be too many visitors today. Never are. There are so many that have no family at all and just sit and stare all day! It's sad, for sure.

"I'd like to go shopping," Mom says.

"Okay, where do you want to go," I asked.

"I guess Lane Bryant's would be good," she said, "but let's wait until tomorrow." *Tomorrow.*

How many tomorrows are there?

16

Cruising

I THINK IT will be fun to tell you about a few of our great cruises in the next two or three chapters!

We have enjoyed many of them over the years and each one, even though we went with the same people, always had some sort of adventure.

Our travel companions come from Chicago.

There's Vern, the dad. I refer to him as "Pops." He has since passed away. Louise, also known as "Bahama Mama," his wife. Diana, their daughter, known as "My Diana." But not so little, right now she is in her sixties. I adore her, and we have a wonderful time together when we are on a cruise.

For ten years, we went on a cruise each year with them. We always had a great time and enjoyed their company very much.

Let's travel to Florida, the first experience I would like to share with you.

"Does everyone have everything?" called Fred from downstairs.

"Yes, I think so!" I responded.

"Let's go!" said Fred to me and Erna (Fred's mom).

We put everything in the car—so we thought—and started our drive to the airport.

We had only been in the new house a short time, so getting everything set took some time.

"I will drop you two off at the terminal and then go to the parking center and be back," Fred told us as we were approaching the airport.

"No problem," I said, "we can get the luggage organized but can't check in until you come back."

"Okay, it won't take long," replied Freddy.

So he dropped us off, and we removed the luggage from the car, and off he went.

As we were getting things together, Erna asked, "Where is my dress bag?"

"I don't know, I didn't pack it. Where was it?" I asked.

"It was hanging on the back of the guest room door," she told me.

"Well, I guess it's still there!" I exclaimed.

Just then Freddy arrived. "Hey, Freddy," I said, "what's Erna gonna wear to dinner on the cruise?"

"I hope some of those new dresses she bought!" he said.

"Well, guess again!" I said. "We left them hanging behind the door!"

"I guess she'll have to buy new ones!" he kind of said.

There wasn't any time to go back; so we went ahead, checked in, and left for Fort Lauderdale. Fortunately, we were going down a few days early to see some sites and then board the ship.

A friend of Fred's from work lived close by. When we got to Florida, he called and told her what happened. She went over, got the dress bag, and FedEx'd them to us at the hotel. But not before having trouble with the house alarm!

Okay, problem solved. Yes! Now to enjoy the vacation!

The hotel in Fort Lauderdale was very nice, and we met up with our friends from Chicago.

We did some sightseeing the next day, went for dinner, and got ready to head out the following day for the cruise. The dresses arrived, pretty expensive deal, and all was good. So you think!

We boarded the ship, settled in to the rooms, and looked for something to eat! Always plenty of that, right?

The ship sailed that evening, and we all went to dinner.

The funny thing about the cruise at dinnertime is that all the older folks are waiting in line to go into the dining room. Like they're not going to get a seat! They have assigned tables!

I guess we were a few days into the trip, and we were all at dinner.

One of the stops was going to be St. Thomas. Great place for shopping, and Bahama Mamma and Erna have this fixation for jewelry! *H. Stern* has a shop there, and Bahama Mamma has a personal relationship with one of the salesgirls. They e-mail each other, and she lets her know when she will be there. They also have policies that if you bought something, you have one year to return it, actually, exchange it, for something else of the same value.

So every year, they buy something new. Bahama Mama actual hyperventilates when she enters the store. Between the two of them, 40k is easily spent on some type of jewels!

We were a few days off that stop by now. We all went to dinner. I think we were on the way to Santa Domingo. Not totally sure. But anyway, we went to dinner and then decided to all go to the show instead of going right for the casino.

That is a bad thing, having a casino right there!

We sat together. We always did. They were just a nice family to travel with, and we did become very close as the years went by.

We were sitting there, and I was next to Pops. He leaned over and said, "Do you have any antacids in your room?"

"Sure, I'll go get some," I whispered.

"No, let me go with you," he said.

"Okay."

So out we went.

When we were outside the showroom, he turned to me and said, "I think you better take me right to the doctor's office, I think I am having some trouble!"

"Ok, come on, Pops, it's not far."

We got there and had to wait a short time for the doc to arrive.

He took Pops in, and a few minutes later he came out.

"Listen, I am sorry to say, but he's having a heart attack!" he said. "Is his wife here?"

"I'll go get her!"

In the meantime, Freddy had come looking for us as he felt that something was wrong, and he came to the office.

"Pops had a heart attack, we have to get Mamma!"

Fred went to get her, and I stayed with Pops. Fortunately, they had this new drug aboard that he injected in, and it basically saved his life! You see, Pops was also suffering from leukemia, which was in remission, and emphysema that really gave him a bad time once in a while.

"Mrs. Parker," the doctor said, "his cruise is over!"

They kept him in the hospital there, and we went to see him. When we got to the next stop, he had to be airlifted off the ship, and they both went to Miami for treatment. He was going to stay there until we got back to Fort Lauderdale. He was doing really well.

"What about my jewelry?" Mamma asked.

Diana stayed with us on the ship, and she had a ball! She is a great sports fan, and one day she was in the sports bar talking with the guys about the games on the screen! Too funny! We let her do her thing as long as she checked in with us during the day so we knew where she was. She really enjoyed herself, and we enjoyed her.

"Fred, here's what you have to do." And Mamma gave instructions about the jewelry and what he had to do with it. I think he was returning something, and they would issue her a credit for next year. Too funny! Worried about the jewels!

All in all, it was a pretty good trip. It was one of the long ones, two weeks, so we really had a good time!

Are you familiar with McCormick Spice Company? Well, next chapter is about one of the heirs to the company and her travels with us. Stay tuned.

17

Magic moments

BEFORE I BEGIN my story, I would like to ask a question to all of you. If you want to answer, great! If not, no problem. Just want to give you something to think about!

Let's travel way back in time. Well, not too far for some. For me, way . . . way . . . back!

Remember yourself as a little child. Think about this and comment if you like.

Tell me a short little note on something that happened between you and a nonfamily member that was a very special moment, something that just was so special to you and what it made you feel like.

For instance . . .

This afternoon we were out to lunch, a welcome thing after not feeling well enough to even get out of bed for a few days. Just in conversation, Fred told us about a very special little moment in his childhood that has been with him all his life. Now, I also have to tell you that he didn't want me to use his name, so forget it as soon as you can! LOL!

His magic moment was when he was a little boy and he loved to go and visit the shoemaker. He would let him play with the machines, the pieces of leather, and the other tools of his trade. And that special time was when the shoemaker's wife would not only prepare a sandwich for her husband, but for him as well. They were a Jewish couple, and his first experience with matzo and cream cheese and olives! This was his, I guess as Oprah would put it, his "aha" moment! They would sit in the workroom, and they would have their sandwiches together.

Mine happened with Louie. I told you about him and Anna earlier. He would run to Delito's market, pick up a small jar of peanut butter, and he and I would sit very quiet on the back stoop and wait for this one squirrel to come and have some. His name was Skippy! What else! It was just us, no Anna, no one else, and it was my "aha" moment! We did this very often, until, I guess, Skippy ate too much peanut butter!

So if you have one, let's hear it!

Now, in the last chapter, at the end, I said to remember McCormick Spices. Correct?

This might become a little scattered, but I will try to make it come together as best as possible.

"Mr. Schneeberg?" said the man on the other end of the phone.

"This is Paul from the Princess Cruise office," he said.

"Yes, what's up?" he replied.

"I just wanted to let you know that you will be dining at the early seating, and you will be sitting with the Parker Family and the Countess.

Fred thought about it a moment, kind of chuckled, and thanked the gentleman for calling.

"Louise!" Fred said as she picked up the phone.

"Yes. Hi Freddy," said Louise, ever so brightly. (She's in love with him!)

"Louise, I just received a call from Princess. They informed me that we would be dining with the Countess!"

"Oh," said Louise, "I did mention that we were traveling with the Countess from the McCormick family."

"Well, wait until they see this!"

They both had a good laugh, and we were scheduled to leave shortly thereafter.

So now . . . the Countess.

She really was a Countess. Really was an heir to the McCormick fortune. Really was royalty. Only thing, she was in her nineties, in care of the Parkers for several years as her son was not interested in taking care of her. She was blind, deaf, wheelchair bound, and couldn't speak! Had to be fed, bathed, and all that's involved caring for an elderly, very sick, woman.

You see, somehow they had befriended her along the way, and they were very upset when her son had decided to put her in a home. At the time, I believe, she was still mobile, and they were taking care of her. They petitioned the courts and gained custody of her and became her full-time caretakers. Now, they weren't young to begin with. This was a tremendous undertaking, but they truly loved her, and they took wonderful care of her! She was always clean, never left alone, and went on almost every cruise we were on. The particulars, I don't know. But I will check and see what I can find out.

Sometime I and Fred would joke about her—just in fun, and only to ourselves.

"I bet when they get back to the room, Renee (that was her name) would say to Louise, 'If you feed me that fish one more time, I'm gonna throw it at you!'" And we'd laugh. It was funny because we always got to do everything first with her—first for dinner, first for anything that she was a part of. Boarding the ship, leaving the ship. It was our number one ticket! But with love!

I give them so much credit for what they did. Renee died during that cruise that I described in the last chapter. It was the first time that they didn't take her, and they left her in a private care facility. We heard that she passed away when we arrived back from the cruise in Florida.

I need to do some additional research on her and report back. She led a very interesting life from what we have heard.

Now we are heading for a really great cruise.

We all decided that Tahiti would be a wonderful place to see as well as Bora Bora, Christmas Island, and Hawaii.

We flew out to California a few days earlier to enjoy some sightseeing before our travel partners arrived. We then all boarded the plane for the flight to Hawaii where we would catch the ship and cruise around the Hawaiian Islands, and then make our way to Tahiti. Beautiful!

Christmas Island, got the vision? Shops? Santa? Reindeer? Great things to buy? Ha! None of the above!

It's an old, basically deserted island, leftover from WWII I believe—very few inhabitants, a small post office, a few shacks and *hot as hell!*

The water around the small island is very shallow, so the tender that we had to take to the ship got stuck in the sand. We had to get out and finish getting to the island by either walking in the shallow water, or I think there may have been some small boats. You have to remember that most of these folks are kind of older, and it wasn't easy for them to get around. Why they wanted to go is beyond me.

It took us about thirty minutes to see what there was to see, and then we had to wait hours before we could get back to the ship! We saw it, floating out there, air conditioned, food, water. Ahhhh . . . out there . . . too far to get to by walking! We had to wait for the tide to come in to get the tenders close enough to pick us all up. Many were suffering from the heat. The ship did manage to bring over cold drinks I think, so it was okay for most of us. Just a long wait in the broiling heat! Not a single holiday item for me to buy. Crap!

We finally made it back and were very relieved to be on board. We headed to our next destination.

Guess what? I made the stupid decision to try to scuba dive! Am I nuts? I hate being under the water, and I am a lousy swimmer!

"No problem!" said Fred. "It's a beginners class, and they're going to suit us up, and we're going to walk in from the shoreline!"

"Hmmmm, I think I can handle that!" I said, apprehensively.

We got to the shore and headed to the dock where we were supposed to meet. They gave us the wet suits, and we put them on. Very slenderizing! Right! I felt like a sausage!

Then, we all got into a boat! *A boat*, I thought. Why is this?

"Why are we going out into the ocean, Fred?" I warbled.

"I'm not sure, but it's going to be an adventure!" he laughed.

Well, out in the most magnificent water I have ever seen we were, floating around in a boat with several other enthusiastic divers!

"Okay, let's suit up, and here is the gear you need to put on," said the instructor.

So I did what I was told, very scared now, very shaky, very nervous. Even though I could see the bottom of the ocean, I had no intention of viewing it close-up! I could see everything just fine from where I was!

"Now, sit on the edge of the boat facing in and roll back into the water," the instructor said.

"No fuckin way!" I said.

"Come on, you can do it!" encouraged Fred.

"No, I can't! You go, enjoy yourself, and I'll watch from here!" I screamed . . . quietly.

Everyone went in, and there was one very, very large man who just wouldn't stay down. They had to add extra weights to him, and I was not impressed with this at all.

The instructor said that he would help me.

"Okay, I'll try," I said.

Into the water I went. I stopped breathing, started to hyperventilate, couldn't get control of anything. Out of the water I angrily came and refused to go any further.

He kind of didn't want to press it anymore and told me that I could snorkel around the boat and he would feed the fish, and I had a good time. There were millions of these tiny fish that swam all around me, and they tickled as they nibbled my exposed flesh, and the scuba . . . well, it wasn't going to happen for me.

We made it back to the ship, and boy, was I glad to get back there!

We continued on a wonderful journey through these incredible islands and enjoyed a super time as we made our way to Tahiti!

And then, the trip home.

18

Tahiti

BEFORE I BEGIN the journey home from Tahiti, I want to let you know this.

I have begun some research on the Countess I spoke about in the last chapter.

Her full name was Countess Renee de Fontarce McCormick!

Pretty impressive, huh?

Well, according to what I have found so far, and it's not much, she did write a few books. One was called *Little Coquette*. It is about the life of a young girl in Paris. As she states in a Web site, it is not necessarily her story, but what she would have liked to have been.

There are others, and I will make that a separate chapter as I gather more information. I am going to ask my friend Louise for some facts and see what we can come up with. I did see that she was born in the late 1890s and died in the late 1990s.

More to follow . . .

Now let's go home from Tahiti! It's been a long trip!

But a beautiful one!

The only problem with going from the West Coast to the East is the fact that you have to leave this island at night. Well, it was supposed to be an early evening flight, but things just didn't go right.

We had to leave the ship and go to the airport. Because we didn't book our entire flight through the cruise line, we really didn't have much flexibility with the times. We were basically at their mercy.

I think the flight was supposed to leave by 8:00 p.m. and get us into Los Angeles in time for an early flight to Philadelphia. We had booked our own flight from there, and we were booked in first class so we could get some sleep. Ha!

We had a long wait at the airport. I just can't remember if we did an excursion and then went to the airport, or we went right to the airport, just not sure. See, that's why I want to write this before I may totally forget!

Anyway, the flight was *delayed* . . . and *delayed* . . . and *delayed* until 2:00 a.m.!

It was on Tower Air, a charter airline that was on its very last flight of its life! That's right. We were on the very last flight that Tower Air was going to have. The last flight from Tahiti to Los Angeles, eight hours.

Eight hours of shaking, rocking, jumping, shaking. *Terrible!* We thought the plane was going to fall apart in the sky, and it was totally packed and the largest plane I had ever been on! I felt like we were flying in a mall in the sky. It was so big!

Even though we were there so early and the plane was so large, we still couldn't sit together.

So we all had aisle seats a few rows apart. Not too bad. I usually prefer a window, but in this case, I was very happy to be on the aisle.

We finally took off, and I thought we would just disintegrate while trying to get up into the air! It was just awful!

Things quieted down a bit once we were airborne, and the movie started. Yes, a movie! After all, it was an eight-hour flight!

They served dinner or breakfast, I don't know which, and everyone started to fall asleep.

But we shook, and we shook.

I had a couple that was seated next to me. There were three seats on each side and five in the middle. The husband was next to me and the wife at the window.

I had fallen asleep for a while when all of a sudden I felt like someone was standing over me! I thought, *This must be it! We're done!*

I opened my eyes, and there in front of me was the husband, attempting to get out of the row.

"Excuse me!" I said. "Just ask, I'll move!"

"I didn't want to wake you, I can make it over you," he exclaimed.

"No, that's okay, I'll move!"

I got up and let him out. The wife was still sleeping. I waited for it seemed like a half hour, and he still didn't return. So I settled in and started to fall asleep again.

Hmmm, I thought.

What's that odor? I said to myself, my eyes still closed and head rolled to the side.

I thought nothing of it and started to go to sleep again.

It's there again! I wonder what it is, I thought.

I slowly opened my eyes, slowly . . . opened . . . my . . . eyes—*why did I do that?*

In front of me, as large as life was an ass! Her ass!

"Hey, what's going on? What are you doing?"

"I'm trying to get out of my seat!" she cried.

"Well, wait until I move!" I said.

"It's okay, I can make it."

By this time, she was almost out and finished her climb as her pants were falling off, and the old fuck didn't even have any panties on! Nothing! Just a pair of sweat pants!

She got out into the aisle and proceeded to bend down to pick up her pants! And guess what? Fred was sitting right behind me. I thought he was further back. But he was right there, and this time, he was the lucky one to have her big fat ass right in his face! He was still sleeping, didn't wake up right away, and missed the big white mass that was attached to this woman!

The people who were awake around us started to laugh and laugh until everyone was awake and wondering what was going on!

This woman never thought twice about this and just pulled up her pants and went about her business. It was so unbelievable! Fred couldn't believe it when I told him when he woke up. Everyone was in hysterics.

Fortunately, they both decided to spend most of the time standing in the rear of the plane, so I didn't have to put up with them the rest of the flight.

Well, to make matters worse, we were very late arriving into Los Angeles and missed our great first-class seats back home. Now what?

I called the USAir service number, and the best they could do was put us on the red-eye back to Philly that night! Yuck! But I had to get back to work.

Remember, we left Tahiti on Monday night or Tuesday morning at 2:00 a.m. We got to Los Angeles and had to wait for the red-eye at 11:00 p.m. on Tuesday night. We finally arrived home on Wednesday morning with the time change. We had been up for two days trying to get home. It may have been a little longer as I have blocked this experience out of my mind. It was really difficult for Fred's mom to travel like this, and I think it took us a week to actually get back in order. It was a nightmare!

A beautiful trip with a not-so-happy ending!

Thankfully, we did get home. What a journey.

19

Growing upon First Avenue

I REALLY FEEL like I need to write more often, but work and home life has kept me busy this past week.

I was down with the flu and then had meetings at work that kept me busy.

I am going to go and visit Mom tomorrow. My brothers tell me that she is just not herself and she asked for me all day today. It worries me when I hear that. I hope she will be okay, and I will keep you posted.

I hope to talk with her a bit, but her sleep pattern is all messed up, so she needs some help with sleeping during the day.

I sure wish I could tell you some of the juicy parts she has shared, but I think I better wait for that.

Perhaps if this turns into a novel someday, I will spill the beans!

But I can't right now. I will just have to keep getting as much info as I can!

Let's go back in time a bit too when I was a little boy.

Now I wasn't such a great kid. I know it's hard to believe for those who know me!

Anyway, I had this thing that I had to have things my way, or no way!

My sister and brother used to cringe when I had to go out with them because I would cry a lot!

One very good family friend used to like to take my brother and sister to the boardwalk on the rides and play games. I always wanted to go, but they didn't always want to take me. When they would try to go without me, look out! He used to call me the fire truck, because I would scream like a siren!

I wasn't really that bad, but I did do some rotten things!

One time, when I was just learning to ride a bike, I used to ride up and down the street. I had a different vocabulary at that time too. I would ride up and down and call everyone a "futtin' asshole!" My mother's neighbor would call her up, "Rita, you have to do something with that kid!"

"What can I do?" my mom cried. "He's just a kid!"

Where I got my language from I don't know. My mother and father didn't cuss, but her sisters did. Well, at least one of them. And no, not my Aunt Marie!

I didn't hurt anyone! I got used to the taste of soap! Nothing really worked on me. It was so much better to wait it out and then ignore me for a while. What can you do!

I grew out of it. I grew up. I did, but I still have a fabulous vocabulary!

I was always fascinated with our neighbors. Many of them were Jewish, and I loved it when there was a Bar Mitzvah! One of my favorite things were melon balls! I was fascinated with them! The melon tasted so much better, and the idea that you could carve a whole watermelon into a basket was terrific! I still like to use the melon scoop when I eat melon today!

Yesterday, I was driving to one of our business units with an associate. We were just chatting and all, and I was telling her about my shirttail cousins in Connecticut! I told her I would write this little story in my next chapter.

My grandfather's brother and his family settled in Bethlehem, Connecticut. It's near Torrington and close to Litchfield.

It's a very small town, and across the road from their property was a wonderful, pre-revolutionary cemetery. I loved walking through there even as a kid.

I used to go up there with my grandfather to visit often during the summer. His brother had a son, and his family was there too. They lived on a lake, and they basically owned almost the whole cul-de sac at one time. They did have row boats and rented them out to row on the lake.

The house was pretty big, but it was actually built into the side of a hill. A hill, not a mountain. The kitchen was on the first level. The living room was one floor up, and the bedrooms were on the third. Eventually, they expanded the house, and there was a wonderful wraparound porch on the second level overlooking the lake.

I had three cousins. I guess they were maybe third or fourth, if there is such a thing. Two boys and one girl.

They had a very strict mom and dad. Their mom was a Jehovah's Witness, so things were a bit different.

They weren't allowed to do anything, nothing out of the ordinary. Nothing. Right.

You know what their favorite thing was? They would row out into the lake and proceed to use cuss words and nasty talk! Nuts, huh?

I thought it was pretty funny. I had to behave there, but I did enjoy going up there, and we would stay for a week or so at a time.

One time, I was out in the boat with my cousin. We'll call her Beth. She was a little crazy, but they were really sheltered there.

Anyway, as we were floating around in the boat, she said to me, "What would you do if I stuck my tongue in your ear?"

"I'd hit ya in the head with this oar!" I answered.

She laughed. I rowed as fast as I could back to shore, never looked back, and was really glad when it was time to go home!

I lost contact with them. She was married several times from what I have heard and also had an abusive husband. Too bad. The boys—I'm not sure what happened.

I found an e-mail address of their mother a few years back. I guess she was an aunt. I used to call her Aunt Wilma. I found this address from the town library. She was a librarian, and I sent her a message. She was happy to hear from me, did remember me, and told me that Uncle Pat had passed away several years ago. You would think they would have called the family to tell them, but everyone had lost contact for so many years.

We e-mailed once or twice. She gave me her daughter's e-mail too. I sent her a message once, and her response was weird, and then her e-mails stopped.

I told Aunt Wilma about things, told her about Mom, the rest of the group. I told her about my life, my dogs, my house, my partner. That was it. I've never heard from her again. Crazy, huh?

20

"I want to go home"

I WENT TO visit Mom yesterday. No matter what anyone thinks, I can definitely see that she is failing. I can see it. More than that, I can feel it.

My brother called the night before to tell me that the doctor was in. Her chest x-ray was okay, her heart looks good, and her breathing is just a little off.

They had to give her a breathing treatment with a nebulizer, and she seemed a little better.

When I arrived there, my sister was with her, and she was still in bed.

"I brought you some cookies and flowers and a little pumpkin," I said. I was actually surprised to see how she looked and that she was still in bed.

What worries me more is that she may want to stay in bed.

"Oh, hi," she said. "How are you?"

"Okay, how are you?" I answered and asked.

"Not good."

"I want to go home," she said.

What she really said was "I want to die now, today."

"I don't think this is a good day," I told her.

"Richard will get three days' off when I go," she said, and laughed.

"I get five days!" said Susan.

"Me too," I said.

Does it sound mean? No, not at all. It's something that you have to do, have to say, and have to discuss.

"I need to get a pair of gold slippers," she told us.

"What for?"

"I'm going to wear my red dress and gold sneakers when I die," she said.

"Okay, we'll make sure you have them," we said.

"Do you want a viewing?' Susan asked.

"Nooooo!" she very clearly stated.

She just wants to go to the church and then up to the cemetery to be with her Whitey!

You have to do this. You have to talk about these things. You have to make light of it. You have to make her feel comfortable with things and to not be afraid; and then, in the car, on your way home, you can cry.

I am extremely grateful for the care that Mom receives from one of the aides. Marcy is a gift from God, and she watches her all the time. Now we do, or I should say, Michael does take very good care of her and make sure that she gets things the others don't. He is very careful on how and when she is rewarded. You have to do this. You need that comfort level when you are not there. She's like the guardian angel that watches over her at night, with the help of God.

Her sleeping pattern is off, and she is awake a lot during the night and then very sleepy during the day.

She sees many familiar things in her life all the time, remembers things that happened, people she know, sometimes doesn't remember that someone died or where they are now.

She'll ask me about certain people every time I am there, and I tell her the same thing. "Okay," she says.

Her roommate was not there when I was visiting.

'Where is this lady?" I asked Marcy as I pointed to her empty, stripped bed.

"She was unresponsive, so she's now in the hospital," she said.

I looked around. I saw her bible, her very few possessions, and wondered if anyone would claim them. I don't think she has any family. I looked in her closet and saw that my mother's halloween sweatshirt was on the floor of her closet.

"She always takes my stuff," Mom said.

"Don't worry about it, I have it now," I said.

"These cookies are awful!" she said, as she ate the second one of the day.

The clothes hang in the closet. The few pictures and possessions sit on the nightstand. Maybe someone will claim them. More than likely, they will be thrown away. Ohhhh, tough.

I think I have said this before, but this is the toughest part of my life. It's so hard to see her lying in bed, unable to care for herself, and at the mercy of someone who will help her at all times. I have a feeling that it will become hard for her to eat by herself soon.

"Why don't you move your right arm, Ma?" I asked.

"I don't know, it doesn't go all the time," she said.

"I think part of my leg is gone, and guess what? Someone took my boobs too!"

"No, your leg is there, but I'm not looking for your boobs!" I laughed!

You have to.

You have to laugh.

You have to joke.

You have to play.

You have to cry.

By yourself.

It's not easy, but you have to.

21

One life changes . . .
with the blink of an eye!

It's TRULY AMAZING how life can change in the blink of an eye.

"My legs and knees are really hurting," I said to Fred one day on my return from a strenuous business trip.

"I better make an appointment with the doc and see what's up," I said to him.

"Maybe he can give you a shot," Fred said.

I had just finished a round of injections in May with a new medicine that was supposed to lubricate the joints and make the knees feel better. It really did help for a few months. It was supposed to last up to a year, but with all the pavement pounding I do at work, it just doesn't last that long.

"I think I'll give you a shot of cortisone in each knee to help for right now," the doc said.

"I want you to get an MRI of your spine. There may be a disc issue that is causing this pain," he said.

"Okay, maybe, let's take a look and see," I told him.

The MRI was scheduled for the next week. Oh how I hate those things!

This isn't too bad as I don't have to go all the way in. It takes about forty minutes, but it seems like years! The banging, the loud sounds that just seem to amplify in this very tiny space!

I got all ready, had the test, and the tech said that he would send over the written report to the doc and he would probably call me on Monday. I had to wait for them to prepare a CD so I could bring that along on my next visit.

All done, all good. Let's go home.

I can't remember exactly which day I went for the test. It was an evening. I think on a Wednesday. I figured it would take several days to read it and then get an appointment.

Didn't work that way, the next day he called.

"Hey, Doctor Schaaf here, I have some results for you," he said.

"Good, that was fast," I said.

"Well, the thing is, the tech saw something on the image, and I am confirming it. You have some type of mass on your right kidney," he very cautiously said.

"What?" I said, somewhat confused.

"My kidney?"

"Yes, and I need you to schedule another MRI just for the kidney. I will have the office prepare the necessary approvals and get you set up. Just call when you receive the information and set the appointment up," he told me.

"Well, okay, I am heading out for a business trip, will do it as soon as I return."

"Okay, just don't wait too long," he said.

Just don't wait too long? What does that mean? What's too long? What's going on?

I received the paperwork in the mail and scheduled it for a week later. That was the quickest they could do it.

I arrived at the hospital in the early morning, six forty-five to be exact. The test was at seven thirty, and it would take about forty-five minutes.

Not only would I have to go almost *all* the way in the f—'n tube, but I needed an IV so they could inject a dye to highlight the kidney.

I wondered how the dye knew where to go? Is there a specific dye for each organ? Does it have directions from a GPS? Who the hell knows!

"Are you all right in there?" the tech asked.

"Yes, doing fine," I said.

Bang, bang, whirl, bang.

Hurry, please, get me out of here. Never, ever, open your eyes! This thing actually grazes your nose as it goes in. And every once in a while, it goes in a little bit more! Hey, cut that out!

It was finally over, and I got to get out.

Once I was out and looking around, I saw that it was actually open-ended. It didn't seem so bad once I saw that. Too bad, I didn't notice in the beginning!

"Okay, get dressed and stop by the film lab and pick up your CD. I'll send the report to the doc, he'll call on Monday," the tech said.

This was Friday.

I went home, was working on the computer. It was about 11:00 a.m. The phone rings.

"This is Doctor Schaff," he said.

"Yes," I nervously responded.

"I hate to tell you this over the phone, but you have a small tumor on your right kidney, and you must have this looked at right away!" he said, nicely.

"What?"

"A tumor?" I said as I covered my mouth and looked up at Fred as he walked by the table.

"Yes, it's very small, but I want you to have this examined right away. Here's the doctor I want you to see down at Jefferson in Philadelphia," he said.

"Can't I go to Phoenixville?" I asked.

"No, I want this guy to look at you. I know him. I know his work. I want him to do it," he said. "I don't want to have you worry, but the worst case is that they would have to remove your kidney so that whatever this is doesn't spread. You can live perfectly fine with one," he said.

"Okay," I said. I was kind of in shock—remove my kidney, *holy shit!*

"Please don't worry about it. Don't lose any sleep over it. It's just something that has to be looked at, and at least it is very small at this point, and no indications point to anything serious yet."

Don't worry, famous last words, right? It's in me. What the fuck is it? Removal of one kidney, step to the front!

So now I was faced with the job of trying to get through to this office in Philly and get an appointment. I called, left a message, no return call, called again, no return call.

A good friend works in the offices there, and I asked her for a better number. I called, finally got a live person—very nice, kind, and accommodating.

"I can get you in at one forty-five on October 11th," she said. "He is out this coming week."

"Okay, great, I'll take it."

"Okay, please call your doctor and have them fax the written report over and then bring the disc when you come for your appointment," she said. "I will be sending out paperwork for you to fill out and bring with you."

"It will take a few hours as you will have to meet with the resident and then see the doctor," she told me.

"Okay, I will call, get the report sent, and bring the CD. Thanks," I said and hung up.

Crap! What the heck? *Remove a kidney?*

Do you know how long ten days seem when you know that an alien is growing inside of you? It seems like an eternity! When is Monday going to get here?

I didn't want anyone to know. I didn't know exactly what it was, and so I thought why worry them.

I thought about it a few days and decided that I had better tell my sister.

After all, I can't tell my mom; and if anyone does after reading this, *God help them!*

I needed my sister to know, needed her to put me on the prayer list, and make this go away!

I did tell my friend at work because I wanted her to know and because she would help me with scheduling the time I needed to be out of the office.

I didn't want to tell my brother Mike as he would lie awake all night thinking about it, and Richard has enough on his plate; and Steve, well, he just doesn't need to know just yet. Susan is our substitute mom, always has been all our lives, so she needed to know.

I received the paperwork in the mail, opened it to review, and thought, *What the hell?*

The questionnaire wanted to know about the latest state of my penis! All kinds of silly questions about insertion, hardness, and other erectile functions! Are we making porn here? What has this got to do with my tumor? Is it related? Didn't think I had any issues down there.

Then, at the bottom of the second page, it said that if I didn't want to answer these questions, I didn't have to! How crazy is that? I guess they are standard things for visiting a urologist! But wait, it gets better!

I filled out what was necessary and gathered everything I needed for the appointment.

In the meantime, Fred had spoken with Susan, and she said that she would be there for the first appointment. I said okay and then realized that we probably wouldn't know anything anyway that day. It was a holiday anyway, and I told her she really didn't have to be there.

I think deep down, Fred wanted someone there. He wanted her there. He asked me if Terry from work would be there. I said no. It wasn't necessary at this point. But I could tell he wanted someone to be there.

So when I saw Susan at my mom's, we made plans for her to come. And Michael . . . and Liz . . . and Dave. Well, they all stayed at the house with Fred's mom, and Susan came with us.

I am very grateful to all of them, and I am happy that they want to be here. It does make it so much better, and my Freddy has the support that he needs too.

We went to the appointment. It was at one forty-five, and they requested that I be there at one fifteen. We all arrived on time. I signed in, and we waited.

I was called in, and we decided that Fred would come with me and Susan would wait in the waiting room. I really wasn't sure what they were going to ask, and I guess I may have been a little embarrassed if they asked something strange in front of her. Silly, I guess.

The nurse aides did all the preliminary stuff. Blood pressure, good. Urine check, good. Temperature, good. Weight, good. *Ha!* All was good.

Then we had to wait again, maybe forty-five minutes more before they put us into a room. Then we waited . . . and waited . . . and waited.

I fell asleep in the chair. We waited. Finally, the resident and a student came in.

"So you're having back pain?" he asked.

I looked at Fred and back at him.

"No, why?" I asked.

"You had a spine MRI, I just thought you had back pain."

"No, I have a spot on my kidney," I said with a slight chuckle!

"Yes, I see that," and he asked a million questions, did a little exam, told us all about what it was and what will happen, and then excused himself and said that the doctor would be in to see where we go from here.

I forgot to tell you that he also took a phone call as we were speaking. Cell phones, yuck!

So we waited and waited, and I asked Fred to go tell Susan what was happening. He was a bit upset by this point. I guess he started to cry when he went out, and so did she. Oh boy.

Finally, the doc came in, very nice man, and he explained all that would happen. *Very optimistic about the entire thing. We will get rid of this. Soon.*

Yes, on November 2nd to be exact!

My next appointment is October 21st, for pre-op and then a liquid diet starting after dinner on October 31st. Halloween!

Trick or treat!

It's just six days until my operation, and I get more scared every day. Everyone tells me to relax, but it's still difficult to think about.

I did make a mistake again and took a peek at the Internet. Too many scenarios, too many things that could happen or may not happen. No more peeking . . . promise.

I did manage to get more Halloween stuff up, and I will take it all down on Monday. One less thing for Fred to worry about.

He does worry, but I need him to get me through this. My sister, brother, and niece will be up too. I will be very well taken care of.

I've already been told that I will not be allowed any excessive bed time. Oh boy, that's what I was looking forward to.

I have everything in order with work and the benefits department; and today, my friend gave me coloring books, crayons, and puzzle books! Plus, some candy! How good is that!

I will check back with more on Monday, when I am on my liquid diet. Yuck!

22

Getting ready

I AM GOING to use this next chapter to just add my thoughts as I get closer to the date of the operation.

One thing I have definitely learned. *Stay off the Internet!*

There is so much information, some good, some bad, some *very* scary!

I looked a bit and decided that it would be better to wait and see for myself—so many stories about what others have gone through, how long it took for recovery, how much pain they were in, how the IV hurt. Yuck!

I actually am more scared, and I mean scared about the incision than actually what is happening! It seems that the healing is a bit long, and depending on what happens, it can take longer than suggested.

It is extremely important to make sure that I take the correct amount of time and do not rush it. I have no intention of *rushing* this for sure!

I was going to head and see my mom this weekend, but she has a terrible cold, and many patients have colds and pneumonia. My brothers and sister and Fred have advised me to stay home until things are better.

I can't afford a cold at this point!

I will, though, make time to see her just before the operation.

If I don't think about it . . . right.

23

My first job

I FIGURED IT would be nice to get away from sickness for a bit, so I'm going to take you back in time. Back to when I turned eighteen and started my work in visual merchandising, then known as display.

I was speaking with a friend from California yesterday. She called to see how things were going and told me how much she enjoys reading this blog. I told her I was running low on experiences, and she said, "Oh, we had so much fun working in the stores, why don't you write about that?"

So here goes.

Eighteen, wow! How about that? I applied for the job at Steinbach's Department store when I was seventeen. About a month before my eighteenth birthday, I was accepted, but then they realized that I had to be eighteen to work in the store for insurance reasons. I figured that was that, but they waited and hired me at eighteen.

I was originally hired to work in the warehouse display where they prepared all the things for the stores. There were, I think, four stores at the time. They would get the major props together there and then send them out to the individual team members in the stores.

But to my delight, there was a person who went out sick, and they let me stay there and fill in.

I guess it also helped that my mom knew the operations manager, and also my cousin worked there too.

So I started in the store in Asbury Park, a very old and beautiful, wonderful, five-floor department store! The one I used to go to as a kid to look at the window displays and dream of working with all the wonderful mechanical figures that graced the windows each year.

How great is this! Well, as I said in an earlier chapter, a fire in the warehouse squashed that dream and all my figures went up in smoke! Up the chimney they rose.

So here I was, fresh out of high school, no formal training—two co-workers that were way above what I could do or dream to do. Yeah. Right.

My first task was to completely change all the felt boards in the entire men's department. These were attached to the tall columns that graced the department and were cut with a fancy edge. No small task to say the least.

Well, their plan was to give me this task, and they would then take the day and leave the store for whatever reasons. I don't know, do I?

Anyway, they planned on this job taking me at least two to three days so they could goof off while I worked. Hey, it didn't bother me. I was loving every minute of it. Even the fact that by the end of the first day, I was finished—yup, all removed, covered, and put back up, I don't think they liked that at all.

They continued to give me task after task, and I continued to finish them, very efficiently, in a short amount of time.

I was very anxious to do good, wanted to not waste any time on things, and make a full day out of the work. I used to run up and down the stairs instead of using the elevators. There was a large staircase on each side of the store, so I could make it in record time. Ahh . . . to be young again.

It didn't take long before I could hardly move my legs, and Aunt Marie suggested and bought me support socks. She also told me to stop walking the stairs and use the elevator.

I loved working there and really made some lovely friends. Even the two that I started with became good work buddies, and it was really enjoyable to go to work each day.

Christmastime was still magical, minus the mechanical windows. It was a process that was unbelievable. The store would close for Thanksgiving, and when the customers returned on Friday, it was all ready for the holiday! We worked through the night to get it ready. We prepared many days in advance, but the big event took place on that Friday, Black Friday as it was known and still is. You couldn't get me near a store on that day now.

I had some interesting characters that I worked with in the store. The best ones were the cosmetic girls—lots of free samples, free product during the holidays. Sometimes they would use us as guinea pigs for new products. We would sit there, and they would apply crap to our faces, and we would laugh and laugh, always before store hours.

There was one customer that was there every day. She would walk up and down the cosmetic counters, and as she did so, chatting with the girls, she would put items in her handbag or shopping bag. A shoplifter! Right in front of your eyes! No one ever stopped her. She had a problem, was kind of old, and her husband would come in and pay for what she took. Too funny. This happened almost every day!

The store was located in Asbury Park, New Jersey, right across the lake from Ocean Grove. Ocean Grove is a small, at that time a very Methodist community, and a very old community. The majority of the customers from there were quite old and were regulars there every day.

You knew them by name, and they knew you. Some of them would come just to watch their soaps on the TVs in the TV department. I would stand there with them and watch. It was always during lunch hour! It was a standing invitation.

In those days, they had elevator operators.

Tina was the operator on one of the elevators that we knew well. She was a very funny middle-aged black woman and had us laughing the moment she arrived until the day was over!

"Hey, watch this," she would tell us. "This woman in here is gonna trip as she comes out of the elevator!" she would say.

Sure enough. Like clockwork, every day, she would trip on her way out of the elevator. Tina thought this was hysterical, but she always looked out for her to make sure she didn't fall.

The fourth floor had a ladies lounge, as it was known then—a really large bathroom that became a meeting place for the older set as they did their shopping. I never could figure out what they were buying. I think most of them just carried the bag around, and this was their activity for the day.

One afternoon, there was quite a commotion up there. We all went up to see what was going on. We stepped off the elevator.

"Sheeeet! It's sheeeeet!" This sales associate screamed in her Indian voice. "It's sheeett . . . sheetttt!"

Well, one of the old ones had lost control and dumped all the way from the elevator to the restroom. Oh boy, what a mess! I felt sorry for the janitor. Later, I found out they had to toss as to who was going to go and clean it up!

Every day there was something, but they had the best hamburgers in the restaurant that I have ever eaten! *The best!* They came from the butcher on the next corner and were fresh every day! I always had two, until the guy I worked with told me that I was eating too much! So I only had two when he wasn't there. Weight wasn't an issue then. I could eat anything I wanted and never gain an ounce. As I said before, to be young again!

I had some terrific teachers while I worked in that store. A fashion coordinator, named Blanche, lovely, wicked woman. Taught me so much, but oh boy, she could rip you apart just with a stare! We became very good friends, and I used to share a cup of tea with her once in a while. She was older than all of us, had a very lonely life, but she was a great teacher and showed me many things about my job that I still use today.

"You know dear, I just didn't blow in today!" she would tell me if I would question anything she told me. Sometimes we would argue, but she always won.

She introduced me to shopping at Lord and Taylor in New York, the soup bar there where you could have wonderful barley soup and a slice of warm apple pie with cheddar cheese! Yum! She was a delight.

One time, when we lived in the same apartment building, she invited me up for tea. She gave me one of her prized teapots and my own cup and saucer to use when we shared tea. I still have it and think of her often.

She passed away a long time ago, but her teaching and memories are still with me.

Well, to tell you the truth, everyone I worked with at that store, except one or two, have passed on. They were old then.

I knew everyone in all departments, and we had such a wonderful time in those days. It was amazing, and I learned, and I became so interested in the job that it still lives on today!

I had this terrific guy that I worked with. I became very friendly with him and his wife outside of work as well. I was there when their twins were born, and we shared so many good times. Every day at three, we would have goofy hour—just screw up things and laugh our asses off. A great guy, a great wife and a terrific family. I'm sorry I didn't remain close, just how things are. He passed away at a very young age of fifty-two or so, just a few years ago. Very sad.

But there was a line he used one day that sent the entire alteration department in a tizzy. These old ladies laughed so hard; I thought they would have heart attacks.

In the alteration room, we were using their sewing machines to make some tablecloths. As he was sewing he said, "Well, she may not have been a good seamstress, but she sure could mend straight!" Get it? Rolling on the floor! I still use it to this day! Priceless!

My other sweet ladies worked in the mail room. They sent out all the packages from the store, and our display room was right next door. We laughed with them every day. Sometimes we would have lunch together.

One was very tiny, very timid, very sweet; the other was loud, wore thick glasses, and had a couple of husbands. Nice ladies, yes.

Now understand that I did and maybe still do have a tendency to use some foul language. Now and then, right?

So one day, Flossie, that was the timid one, came to work. She was kind of sad, and very quiet.

"What's wrong, Flos?" I asked.

"Hmm, you got me in trouble last night," she said quietly.

"Me? Why?" I asked.

"Well, my husband said something that I didn't like, so I told him to go fuck himself!" She started laughing.

We almost wet the floor with laughter!

God rest them all. We had fun.

24

My mentors

Do we ever stop working? It seems like we wait and wait for school to be over. Now we wait and wait for work to be over. Then what?

So I must say, as I did in the last chapter, working with the people I did in the very beginning of my career molded me and taught me great things.

Hank Barrett, Blanche King, Jim Elliott and Patrick Pescatore were the best teachers I ever had.

Each one had his own style, his own methods and his own values.

Each one taught me, molded me, and sent me off in the right direction for what I wanted to do, was good at, and most important, love doing!

My dad always said that if you love your job, it makes it much easier to get up and go to work every day!

I think the two that stuck in my mind most are Blanche and Patrick.

Blanche was our fashion coordinator. She was the one who decided what the current trends would be for the store, what the window fashions would be and how we put all this together.

She had a wonderful approach to pulling the entire outfit together—the right colors, fabrics, styles and the correct accessories.

"No, dear, not that belt. Let's try this," she would tell me.

"But I like this one with this," I would answer.

Only had to get the "look" to know that I lost that fight!

She also used to write down all things that were of interest to her during the day—whether it was a special word, a phrase, a look, or anything that she wanted to remember. She always carried a small notepad with her, and she had the most wonderful, unique handwriting—kind of like printing and writing at the same time. Beautiful!

She taught me the correct way to add color and textures to make an outfit complete. Funny thing, she was only really interested in the female mannequins, and we were kind of left on our own with the males. We didn't have too many of those though.

She had a unique way of pulling it all together and telling a story with your eyes. The shoes, even the stockings were perfect.

This has been very helpful with me teaching my coworkers in all the stores we have now, and I was able to pull from my memory when I created our visual manual that is still in use today.

I can still hear her bangles bracelets clanging when she was trying to make a point and shaking her long, beautiful, perfectly manicured hands at us. She never stayed mad for more than a minute. Priceless.

One thing that used to amaze me, she would go to New York often—to the markets and to the stores. In the winter, now get this, she would put newspaper in her coat, the back part, to keep the wind and cold out! Only a classy woman could pull that off!

Patrick, a good friend and coworker.

His ability to work in the home areas was exceptional. I know he was instrumental in my development in that department.

House wares, furniture, home accessories—anything related to that section. Linens, bedrooms, all fun and exciting to work in.

We would do all kinds of things with sheets—draperies, wall covers, anything that would pull the whole thing together.

We had one very large corner window that we used to devote to home furnishings. That was the fun time. He would show me how to build bed frames, fabric covered and padded, matching cornice boards, bedspreads, bed skirts, the whole thing.

I think we are all born with abilities. We just have to sharpen them as we get older and then take that and teach others.

He showed me how to balance rooms, coordinate colors, and use the right accessories, the best paint colors, and how to pull it all together.

All of these things and much more are part of me, and I continue to use them in my current role.

I stayed with Steinbachs for about eight years before I moved on to Abraham and Strauss.

I worked in Asbury Park, Bricktown, and Mays Landing for Steinbachs.

Abraham and Strauss, a Brooklyn-based company was advertising for a visual director at their Monmouth Mall store. I think this was in '81 or so. I applied for the job and was accepted.

It was close to home, and a fairly new store—much larger than I was used to and a bigger department. I went from working by myself to having three people report to me. It was strange but challenging.

I still was more interested in working in the home areas more than fashion, but I must say, I was a snazzy dresser then! Oh yeah! Sometimes strange, but snazzy!

I think one of my all-time favorite outfits actually was worn when I still worked for Steinbachs. Now, picture this—blue and white checked shirt, cotton, one-half-inch square check, matching pants (that's right, matching pants), white shoes, and to end it all, blue and white shoelaces! *Yes!* I did wear that! At work, in the store! Gorgeous!

I was much thinner in those days at A&S, so I was able to wear all kinds of things. I was so thin that I could actually fit into a pair of teen-size khaki pants from the junior department! They were exactly like the men's, only more colors! So I had all different-colored pants, matching polo, and cloth belt and socks. Yeah, socks. What a freak!

I had a store manager, Nick Kangos, and an operations manager, Jim Davis. They were always looking for me to do something. They were always competing with each other, and I was in the middle.

I remember as if it were yesterday. There were three floors to this store. I was on the middle escalator one morning, over the top screamed Jim for me and down below screamed Nick. I went straight ahead!

I will say that I didn't have as much fun once I left Steinbachs, but I did continue to learn my trade from some great teachers again. The fact that A&S was based in New York gave me a whole new perspective on fashion, for the home as well as the body—more detailed and much more to know about the current trends.

They had five or six stores, and we all had plans to follow monthly for our displays. We all had the freedom to add our own touch, but we all had the same basic setup. We all pitched in with Christmas decorating and helped each other out.

I started in Steinbachs when I was eighteen. I moved to A&S when I was twenty-four. I changed to ARAMARK, back then ARA Services, when I was twenty-eight.

I remember telling my Aunt Annie, "I'm only twenty-eight, now's the time to move on."

"Yes, just don't hop around too much," she said.

Well, twenty-four years later, I'm still at ARAMARK!

25

Pa Bound

"GET THOSE F—'N Foo dogs outta that front window now!" screamed the VP of Visual.

"Why?' I questioned, "They work great here!" I protested.

"Mel hates those and having them right at the entrance is a *really* bad idea!" she exclaimed.

"Oh, poo on him, what the hell does he know?" I yelled.

"Just move 'em!" she hollered and walked away.

We were in the middle of getting our new store in Willow Grove, Pennsylvania, up and running. Tensions were running high, and everyone was a critic!

Mel was the VP of the whole company, and we basically had to satisfy his comments even though most of the time they were crap!

People would shake in their pants when he was coming for a visit. Everything had to be perfect. Really now, it should be anyway, right?

The thing that made me laugh when he would visit is that they had to make sure there was bologna there for his lunch! Bologna! And he knew about Foo Dogs? Ha!

He was always very happy with the work I and my coworker and friend Bob did. He always took the time to say hi and to critique what we had worked on, especially in the home area. That was both our strengths.

He would be so critical that we always knew we had to be ready.

One day he asked why the light was hanging so low over the dining table.

"That's the correct height," Bob said. "If you sit at the table, put your elbow on the table and the bottom the chandelier should just lightly graze the tips of your fingers," Bob explained.

Sure enough he sat there and tried it out, worked just fine, and he left us alone.

We also knew that he was intimately involved with one of the buyers too, but his wife didn't! Well, maybe she didn't.

We had a wonderful crew that we worked with in that store—lots of fun, good people who I enjoyed both in and out of work.

It was my first time with moving away from home at a distance. So I had very limited funds, and it was a real struggle.

My friend Bob and I decided that it would be more cost-effective if we shared an apartment. At that time, he worked in King of Prussia, and I was in Willow Grove. It worked out good, we lived in KoP, and I would drop him at work and then head to Willow Grove. It was about twenty minutes up the turnpike. Then I would pick him up on the way home.

I guess he was on the bad end. He had to go to work earlier than me and wait for me to pick him up!

But that was okay. It gave him less time to move the apartment around.

He was famous for moving furniture all around the place. Nothing was ever in the same place. Sometimes it wasn't even in the same room!

I remember that I was cooking once, he didn't like to cook, and he shut me in the kitchen for several hours. This was due to all the furniture that was in front of the door!

He just loved furniture and was always bringing home something different. It was crazy.

One time he bought this gorgeous white sectional sofa.

"Hey, I thought it would be fun to have the gang over while they are here opening the store," I said to him.

"Sure, why not, what will you have?" he asked.

"I was thinking of baked ziti," I said.

Now, there wasn't any dining room to speak of, so everyone would have to eat wherever. He looked at me, looked at the sofa. "Baked ziti?" he said, kind of scared.

"Oh, right," I said.

But all worked out and not a spot on anything! Red wine too!

Bob was transferred back to Jersey, and I decided to move closer to Willow Grove. Too far to drive every day and I didn't want to be on the turnpike. Even though it was close, traffic was bad most mornings.

I found a house apartment in Ambler, not too far from the store. Really nice old mansion and I had the front first-floor apartment. I also had complete use of the entire enclosed front porch. The only thing was the kitchen was once a coat closet! Not the place to cook for too many! No problem though, money was very tight, and now I had to have a car too.

So I called my cousins in Paoli, John and Carol, and they helped me move to Ambler. I remember that I had to tie the mattress on the top of the car and didn't have any rope. I did a bad thing . . . I went back to the apartment and cut the cord from the venetian blinds! Terrible thing!

But we made it. I had to leave everything there. It was on a Thursday. You can't move into a new place on a Friday. Very bad thing to do in the eyes of the Italians! Never move on a Friday!

It was Easter weekend, so I left it all and went home.

Home—home it always was as long as Mom was there.

I guess I lived there for about a year when I decided to move into Center City. It was a pretty easy ride to Willow Grove and some of the others lived in the city.

I found a great apartment—one room, small kitchen, and a bathroom so small that if you farted in it, you would end up in the next apartment!

But it was safe place, second floor, walk-up, very old but beautiful street in Philly.

It took me about a year to finally get it the way it should be, efficient, yet not crowded. It wasn't a big room, but it did have a larger kitchen than before and two big closets. I also had access to the attic.

One time I decided that I wanted to make a small tiled table to use for dining. I bought a piece of heavy plywood and went around to some of the old antique shops to look for tiles.

I found this old place. They had a few tiles, but the owner told me that he had boxes of old tiles in the basement.

"Go down and pick out what you want," he said. "They've been there for years!"

I saw the dirty old wet boxes and figured out how many I needed. I went through all of them to find enough that were in good shape.

I carried them up. "How much?' I asked. I was hoping he would say free.

"$85 should do it!" he said.

$85?" I cried. "I spent hours picking them out, and you didn't even know what was there!"

"$85," he said again.

"Keep 'em!" I said and walked out, all dirty and dusty from the basement. Old fuck can have his tiles. I couldn't find a single place that had what I wanted. I looked all over.

I finally went back and got him down to $50. Made a great table!

I really loved the street, and it was really close to everything I needed.

I was there about a year when I had a new job offering. It was with ARA Services, based out of the Philadelphia airport. The store manager that I worked with at A&S went there and asked me and a few others to come with him. It was a good opportunity, and I wanted to stay in Philly.

I accepted the job, got screamed at by my store manager because she didn't want me to leave, but went anyway.

I stayed in the apartment a little longer and then decided that I would like more room. I was making a little more money then and thought it would be nice.

I found a great second floor place around the corner and down the block. It was a great old house, and there were only three apartments. I had the second floor and the front of the third floor, fireplace and decent kitchen.

When I met with the owner, she was happy to have me there, and we talked about the rent. I don't know if I had a stroke at that moment, or I just wasn't listening. I thought she said the rent was $475. I thought, well, that's okay. I should be able to do that.

So when it came time to sign the lease, it was only then that I saw that is was actually $675!

Now what the hell am I going to do?

"I thought you didn't understand me when I explained. In order to have the third floor as well, it was $675. I don't have time now to close off the floor, so if you want to back out, I'll let you."

She was really nice about it.

I knew I couldn't afford it, but I really wanted to live there. So I called Bob.

"Hey, do you want to share a place downtown?' I asked. "It's an easy drive to Willow Grove from here."

"Okay, that's a good idea," he said.

What I really didn't tell him was the rent. I told him it was $600, so he paid the $300 and I paid the $375. Why, I don't know.

Then the first floor one became available. It also was included the back part of the second floor. Two bedrooms, two baths, living room with fireplace, *big* kitchen, room off the kitchen, dining room, and front room. Lots of space!

Too much space because he started to fill it up with all his belongings, and before you know it, it was like a museum!

He bought this bed from the store, and it was so big that he had to make his bedroom in the front room because it wouldn't fit upstairs! Too funny.

We had a great time there though, hosted many events and always had weekend company.

My darling friend from New York, now California, would come for the weekend. Viv!

I met her while working at Willow Grove. She came to help open the new store. She worked in Manhasset store in New York, I think.

I knew she was great as soon as I saw her. She was wearing a Barbra Streisand t-shirt! We were friends from that day on!

She used to marvel at all the cooking I would do, and I had this wonderful pantry in between the kitchen and dining room.

She called it the "Magic Closet"!

"What the hell is there?' she would ask. "Anytime you need something, in you go and out comes everything you need!" She loved it!

The woman who owned the house was an attorney for the city, a nice Jewish girl, not yet married, a bit of a whiner, but generally very nice.

So in my usual fashion at Christmas, I went nuts doing the outside of the house. I did the two front windows and the entire front door.

"Hmmm," she said, "this looks great, but since I'm Jewish, can you please tone it down? I would like it if you would remove all the stuff from the front door. You can leave the windows alone, please."

"No problem, sorry for not realizing," I said.

I can't begin to tell you how many times the furniture was moved around, from room to room, from floor to floor! It just was amazing.

It was great though.

26

Getting ready . . . Pre-op

10-3

No, that's not the baseball score. That's the time it took to get all the pre-testing completed for my upcoming hospital stay!

"Good morning, please sign in and wait until you're called," said the receptionist at the front desk.

I signed in, looked around, and was very happy that there wasn't a crowd.

I wonder why I have to be here for three hours, I said to myself.

It's just supposed to be a few tests, and off I go.

"Peter Kay," said the attendant, "Follow me."

Hmm . . . that didn't take long.

"Please wait in here, someone will be in shortly," the guy said.

"Okay, I'll be here," I told him.

This place is amazing. The Jefferson Hospital has bought almost every building around the main hospital and turned it into some type of office. It is a teaching hospital, so they do have many departments and tons of people working here.

It was ten fifty on the clock. I had to be in a different office by one.

11:00 . . . 11:15 . . . 11:30.

"Hello, I'm Dr. (whatever). I'm going to get started on some information."

We proceeded to do the usual. Blood pressure, a bit high, so she said. Last week it was 117/76. Now it is 146/81. I still believe that when they take it over clothing, it's never right.

Weight, height, age, date of birth, and lots of history needed to complete the whole thing. (Notice I didn't tell you my weight?)

11:55

"The girl will be in to take your labs shortly," and off she went.

Now, they are very nice, not pushy or nasty. That makes it better. Yes?

I think I dozed off in the comfy chair for a few.

12:45

"I am here to take your blood," she said.

"I have to be at the cardiologist at one. Will I make it?" I asked.

"You still need an EKG, but you'll be okay," she said.

I heard a cart coming down the hall and figured it was the EKG machine. Sure enough.

"I'll come back in a few," and off she went!

Five tubes of blood later . . .

12:55

"I'm here to take the EKG," said the woman.

"Listen, I'm supposed to be across the street to see the cardiologist at one. I need to also bring the EKG readout," I told her.

"You'll make it, I'll call over there," she said.

She called, told them I would be on my way, and proceeded with the test. It takes longer to stick those things on the hairiest part of your body than actually take the test.

1:05 . . . Finished.

I checked out, got the report, and headed across the street.

Once again, I had more papers to fill out and then wait. It is now close to one thirty. I still have to go down the street to the main hospital and get a chest x-ray.

I am starving. I need something to eat and soon.

I was called in at one forty and met with the doc. All is fine. It took about five minutes for him to read the EKG and be able to make a report back to the surgeon that I am cleared for surgery. The nurse took my blood pressure there too. 117/70. Both arms. Go figure.

Great! I have to head to the hospital for my x-ray. Should I eat first . . . no, I'll wait. Maybe there's a line.

Up to x-ray . . . no line, few minutes' wait, and off I go!

Pizza!

I forgot to tell you this. When the first nurse practitioner met with me back at 11:00 a.m., she said that I was there for a prostate operation. I thought, *Wtf! Is she nuts?*

I only hope that when I do actually go in, that they make a mistake and do liposuction on my belly and a nice face lift! What are the chances of that?

All in all, it wasn't bad, just a lot of running around, but all is done . . . now, wait, one more week! Yikes!

I will admit. I did a stupid thing. I looked on the Internet. Oh boy.

4 days . . .

Have to go for a new chest x-ray this morning. The first one wasn't clear, so off we go to Philly for a new one! They wanted me to come there on Monday. How? Have to drink that stuff to clear me for surgery!

3 days and counting . . .

Went down to Jefferson yesterday for a redo on the chest x-ray. She said all is clear! Good news there!

Today is Sunday and after dinner starts the clear liquids—Jell-O, broth. Fred is making chicken broth as I write, Jell-O too!

Thankfully, I can also have coffee, no cream, Gatorade . . . should be fine except for the magnesium citrate or something like that. That's tomorrow at noon. Getting ready for the Halloween trick or treaters. Have candy bags ready.

I'll check back tomorrow.

2 days, actually one . . .

Monday, almost Tuesday, just had the wonderful magnesium citrate cocktail! Delightful!

Hopefully will know what time I need to be there sometime today.

I think I'm ready. Nervous energy has allowed me to take down all the Halloween stuff, clean up a bit, and get the porch furniture ready for storage.

Seem to be a bit nervous. Oh well, my angels are watching over me.

Tuesday

Heading in at 5:30 a.m.!

To be continued!

27

The Operation

ON MONDAY NIGHT, November 1st, I called the hospital line to see what time we needed to be there the next day. Certain sources said it may not be until 11:00 a.m., and I thought that would be good. I won't have to be up too early, although, the earlier the better, less time to think about it.

"Mr. Kay," said the person on the phone, "you are scheduled for 7:30 a.m. We'll need you here by 5:30 a.m. to get signed in."

Yikes! 5:30 a.m.! Oh well, early will actually be better.

"Come on, Freddy, we have to go," I said in the early morning as we prepared for the ride to Jefferson in the city, a nice thirty-five-minute ride to get my mind in order.

We parked where we were told and walked across the bridge to the admitting area. I think there were about fifty people there already!

I signed in and waited to be called. It didn't take long, and off we went.

First to the room to get signed in and all questions answered. Fred was allowed to come with me at this point.

"Please put this gown on, and when you are through, open the curtain and someone will be right with you," said the nurse.

I changed my clothes. Fred put everything in the bag we brought along.

"Fred, go out and see if Michael is here," I said. Michael said he would be there early, and Susan and Liz and Dave were also on their way.

Michael was there and was allowed to come in too.

"Did you tell them that you were anxious and could use a little boost to get you relaxed?" he asked.

"I'm fine, I don't want anything yet," I answered.

The admitting girl arrived and finished her work. The "anestithist" arrived and then *he* came . . . the one to take me to the holding room for the operation.

It was about a four-to-five minute ride on the gurney to the area where I need to be.

We arrived at the door. I was a bit scared. I said my *so longs* to my Freddy and Michael and went through the doors!

I get all choked up even now.

I was the first one in the room, seemed nice and quiet. They did one IV in my hand and said the rest would be done after I was asleep.

Before I knew it, the place was full! It was now about 7:15, and I had been waiting for about forty-five minutes in there.

Jefferson is also a teaching hospital, so there were lots of people around. Each one of us had our own "anestithis" and assistant.

The resident came in and explained a few things, and then a few minutes later, the doctor arrived. He marked my area that was going to be operated on and said some kind words, and off we went—sleep, sleep, sleep. Wow!

At this point, all I remember is looking at the clock. 7:29.

Did I spell "anestithis" correct?

28

Waking up

I HAVE NO idea what time it is or where I am. I think it's about four in the afternoon or so.

I am being transported to my room on the transplant floor, a private room at that! Thanks to my friend that works there!

Fred, Michael, and Susan are here.

I'm pretty groggy, been in the operating room for five and a half hours! Wow! Did they do a tummy tuck? Eye lift? Probably not!

"Did I die?" I wearily asked Fred.

"No, cause if you did, I did too!" he said.

"Does anyone here have a stethoscope?" asked the nurse to her partners.

"Ask Herman, he has one!" I answered. Big laugh!

I was really out of it, tubes connected, catheter, drain, and . . . *morphine!* Yes! A drip . . . in my control! Yeah!

I didn't realize that Michael was doing a video of me on his phone. I am trying to figure out how to upload for viewing on here. Hopefully, I will figure it out!

I tried to sleep after everyone left, but it seemed like every five minutes, someone was coming in to check something.

"I'm here to check your vitals," the perky nursing assistant said, many, many, many times during the night.

No food yet, good thing, I wasn't even hungry or thinking about it! Just the mere thought made me feel ill. I was thirsty, but not allowed anything but a sip of water now and then. They didn't want me to pee too much I guess. I did have that tube attached to my buddy, and I never even knew if I went or not.

The one assistant gave me a small pitcher of water, and the nurse had a cow! "Who gave you this?" she said.

"I don't know, it was just there when I woke up," I said. Ha!

My room was located right next to the ice and water machine. I can't believe it! I always request a room away from the elevator, the ice machine, and the vending whenever I travel! Yikes!

All night, ice, water, refrigerator door slams, ice, water, slam—all night long, even with the door closed.

My inner temperature was out of whack too! One minute I was sweating, and the next freezing! My head was wet. My feet were ice. I went from the bed to the chair to the bed all night long once I was able to get up!

'Okay, time to get you out of bed," said the nurse from the doctor's office.

"I don't know if I can," I quietly said.

"Yes, you can. We have to get you moving to get that gas out of you," she said. She really was very kind.

I did have terrible reflux, and I couldn't even keep the apple juice from running up and down. I finally asked for something, and the Nexium really helped.

This was only day 2. I had to get out of bed. My big fat ass and the rest of me *had to get out of bed*! Why? I'm okay here!

"Turn to your side and let your legs slide to the floor and then lift," requested the nurse.

Easy for you to say, I thought. Well, not exactly, but I really was watching my mouth and didn't want to say anything bad.

It actually was okay. Not easy, not comfortable, but I did get into the chair.

Still no appetite, just drink, not much, just enough to wet my lips and mouth. Mmmmmmmm, good, water never tasted so good!

Fred and Susan and Liz and Dave arrived in the afternoon. They were heading back home from there, and Fred was staying for the rest of the afternoon.

"It's freezing in here, can't we open the curtains?" he asked.

"I'm sweating. The window opens to the atrium, and everyone can see in," I said. "Sometimes I have to get up, and my ass is hanging out!"

"So what, you're in a hospital!" said Freddy.

"I just can't get cool. I sweat in my head, my feet freeze, but not enough to cover them," I said.

"Well, I'm freezing. I'll put my jacket on, and let's turn the lights on. This isn't a morgue!" bellowed Fred.

"You need to eat," he said.

"I'm not hungry."

"Well, you have to eat to make your body functions work or you can't go home!" he said, like a doctor!

"I will, I just can't right now."

The next day, they brought in some light breakfast.

I tried, but it just wasn't time yet. I ate the Jell-O. I never thought Jell-O could taste so awful! I couldn't even drink the juice as it tasted like I was drinking liquid sugar!

The resident arrived first thing in the morning followed by the bloodsucker!

"I need to take your blood for testing this morning," said the tech.

"Okay, but my hands and arms are pretty swollen," I said.

I'll get it, he thought.

Oh my, my fingers and hands were twice the size, and I could hardly make a fist. They were swollen all the way up my arms and not a vein in sight. I usually have no issues with giving blood, but not this time. He actually couldn't do it. He had to send in the nurse, and they finally found a vein near my thumb. Yikes!

This happened three times in two days. I am black and blue all the way up my right arm. I had two IVs, one in each hand. They still hurt today.

The doctor came in.

"How ya doing," he asked.

"Feel okay," I said.

"Everything went very well, we did a different incision, and instead of going across the ribs, I went below. Less pain in recovery, but it did take longer in the operation. All seems to be fine, I will have the results of the biopsy when you see me in two weeks," he said.

"Okay, thanks. When can I go home?" I asked.

"I think we can plan on Friday, day after tomorrow," he said.

"Okay."

I was now supposed to eat something. They brought my lunch tray, and I had all I could do from throwing up! The smell sent me nuts!

"You have to eat!" Fred said.

"I can't . . . it smells awful!" I cried.

"Just try, please," he asked.

"I'll try the Jell-O and piece of cake."

I think it was a piece of cake. Most of it didn't go anywhere.

"If you don't eat, ya can't go home!" Doctor Fred said.

"I will tomorrow," I said.

29

The days ahead!

WEDNESDAY NIGHT WAS probably the longest night of my life!

I decided that I wanted to sleep and got all ready for bed by seven. I took some pain stuff. The drip was now gone. I settled in and fell right to sleep!

Slam! Ice! Water! Slam! Ice! Water!

I woke up hearing all the noise and felt like I slept a long time! Thank God. I am sure it's near morning, if not already. They don't have clocks in the room, so I had to either turn on the TV or try to look at my watch that Fred brought.

I thought I would shit! It was only 10:00 p.m.! Ten o'clock! I had the whole friggin' night ahead of me.

So in the bed, out of the bed, in the chair, out of the chair . . . "We need to check your vitals" went on all night—all night.

6:00 a.m.

"I need to take your blood," said the man at the door.

"Again, you just took it yesterday," I said.

"I know, but we need it. The last one was tainted because it was taken from the IV area," he said with apology.

"I don't have any veins left, my hands and arms are so swollen," I said, sadly.

"I'll look around and see what I can find." He did, several times, but finally got enough.

Back to sleep, right. "Need to check your vitals!" Yeah!

"Deep breath!" she said.

"I can't go too deep, it's kind of sore," I said.

"Your oxygen level is a bit low, deep breaths should bring it up," she told me.

It seemed like the more I talked, the better the level got. I was convinced at that point that if I went home, all would be better. Better food, better rest, and maybe the ability to sleep.

"Good morning," said the student from the doctor's office. "How are you feeling today?"

"Better, thanks, want to go home," I said.

"Okay, probably Friday. Have to take out that catheter first," he said.

"Okay, good, will it hurt?" I asked.

"No, won't feel a thing" as he pulled what seemed like a mile long tube out of my buddy. Yikes!

Well, it really didn't hurt, just a weird feeling. Now I have to pee by myself into a urinal if I can't get to the toilet, and I can't get to the toilet by myself!

So no issues, no problems, peed and peed . . . all was good so far.

"Hello," said the nurse practitioner. "Time to remove the drain"

"Oh great, another tube out!" I said.

"Okay, now, take a deep breath and exhale" *Whoosh* . . . out it came!

Really, no pain or discomfort. After all, I was still numb there!

"Keep the bandage on, change it daily, and then after a few days just use a band-aid, should be no issues," she told me.

And thankfully, no problems.

Now we still just had the oxygen level thing to worry about but as the day went on, it got better. I still had the tube in my nose, and they told me to keep it there until further notice.

All was good, thank God and St. Theresa!

I still couldn't eat, tasted awful although Freddy thought it was good.

"Eat, or you can't come home," Fred said.

"You eat it, tastes like crap!" I said.

"I know once I get home, I will be able to eat," I said.

Okay, now it's nighttime—well, at least seven again. I have another longest night ahead of me. Crap.

I put my noise-cancelling earphones on this time and was able to sleep a little better, this time from seven to eleven, then up and down all night between the bed and the chair!

It's Thursday morning.

"Morning, I need a blood sample," said the tech.

"Good luck with that one," I whimpered.

He got it, so happy.

The practitioner came in. "How are you?" she asked.

"Feeling pretty good today, better if they stop taking blood!" I said.

"Well, I didn't order blood today, but you'll be out of here tomorrow," she said.

She went over all instructions and had the nurse fill out all the paperwork, and as soon as the blood work came back, she would sign the release forms. Yeah!

Uneventful day and a long and miserable night!

Friday morning, supposed to be out by 10:00 a.m.

Fred would be here soon.

Terry and Len came from the office and brought me a coffee and donut holes. The coffee was great, one donut was enough.

"I'm going home as soon as Fred gets here!" I said as I waited on the edge of the chair.

Oh, I forgot the best part. One of the other reasons that I couldn't go home was because I didn't do a poop! Well, I finally did, not in my pants, in the toilet. Yes! I'm on my way!

Terry and Len left. My boss was there the day before and wanted to bring me food. I just couldn't eat. Even though the pizza shop was right across the street!

I cleaned myself up the best I could. They said I could shower, but I wanted to wait until I got home.

I dressed in my sweats and sweatshirt and even carefully put on my socks. I was all ready when Fred arrived.

The nurse called for transport. We had to wait over an hour!

Finally, I was in the car, going home. I cried a bit. I didn't die. God isn't ready for me yet. Thank you! All in all, I was very fortunate to have this found and to have it found at this stage. Lab report is due on the twenty-second. Stay tuned!

Check-up!

Back from the doctor and all is well!

Yes, it was cancer, but all seems fine at this point. No glands were removed and no follow-up treatments.

They will continue to monitor me with a scan in three months and then once a year to include chest x-rays.

All in all, it's good news. God isn't ready for me yet!

And I'm not ready either.

Peace to all!

30

Thanksgiving

THANKSGIVING, A TIME to give thanks and to gather around family and friends, I guess we should do that all year long, don't you?

But it's a great time of the year, and it's the official start of the holiday season and great times ahead!

So for the last twelve years, we have hosted Thanksgiving at our house. We have had as many as twenty-five and as few as eleven. That was this year.

The first time we did twenty-five, what were we thinking! Oh boy! It was so much work, so much prep time, and so much cleaning up time. Did we learn from that? Nope. We did it again that next year, and then, the light went off, and that was it!

Now we fluctuate between eleven and fifteen depending on who is around.

My dad has a sister. She is ninety-three. The last from his side. She loves to come here for Thanksgiving dinner, and we enjoy having her here with my two cousins, their spouses and in-laws. Always have a nice time and always a relaxing kind of day!

Way too much food, way too many pies, but what can you do.

In 2008, my mom fell, and that was the end of having her here with us as well. It was actually in 2006 that she started to go with my brother and then my sister. Now, she is in the home. My brothers go and have dinner with her. My sister brings her favorite part of the turkey, the wing, and all is good. Well, as good as it can be. I really don't think she knows what day it is all the time, and Thanksgiving is not up on her radar screen.

It may sound mean, but it makes it easier knowing that she kind of isn't sure of the day or if she is, it doesn't bother her. As long as her boys are there, all is good with her.

She's getting frail, quiet. Sometimes, it's getting sad.

I haven't been there in over a month due to my operation but will be heading there next week. Even if you are there every week, she may tell someone she hasn't seen you in months! Oh boy.

We grow up with tradition. We went to my Aunt Sue, my father's sister, for Thanksgiving for many years. I can remember my mom getting her hair done in a French twist, us getting all dressed, and heading to north Jersey for dinner.

Cousin Barb would play the piano. Uncle had a short-wave radio, and we always had plenty to do, and it was always nice as much as I can remember.

Then after my dad got sick, we would have it at home. Aunt Sue and family would come to us, and we would continue our tradition. Always had something going on.

One year, as they drove up, Aunt Sue said, "Am I seeing things, or is that a horse on the lawn?"

Well, sure enough, it was a horse! Back then, my sister was in love with horses. So her boyfriend at the time was in hot pursuit and decided to give her a horse! A horse, a real live overgrown huge horse!

Well, I guess it helped because they did eventually marry . . . still married after thirty-five years!

I remember one time for Christmas my mom thought she was being funny and told my sister she was getting a horse. Instead, she got a small plastic one and hung it on the tree.

From what I can remember, it wasn't such a good thing!

But we had many more good ones as the years went on. We all were together and enjoyed the day. It was also my father's birthday. He was actually born on Thanksgiving, and that was the celebration day no matter what the date was.

So now, as we reach the older years, we have all kind of drifted. My sister is not happy about this at all. But I think it is very important for all of us to have or start our own traditions. Each one of us has a different life, different friends, different ideas. It's important for you to do what works for you.

The love and family will always be there, but the traditions will change.

New ones will be born, new ideas will unfold, and new traditions will become a part of our lives.

They are going to change, all the time. They will change by death, by needs, by sickness, by where you are in the world at any given time. New traditions, they will happen!

I tell my sister. You have your kids. They now have kids. Your life changes. You took over when Mom couldn't. Your daughter will when you can't, and so it goes.

Sometimes they don't change for the best, but they do change, and we have to accept that and move on. That's what makes us all different, all exciting in our own way, our own ideas, thoughts, dreams, and desires.

We all have so much to be thankful for each and every day! Many things, and many things change. There's that word again—*change*. It changes, every single day.

There are so many wonderful family and friends that are no longer with us, and that is change, not always good, but change.

Go with it and enjoy every single day of your life!

31

Christmas memory

I would like to share a quick memory with you that may give you a bit of a chuckle!

"What's that banging noise?" I said to Mom.

We were visiting her at her apartment that she shared with her sister in Asbury Park just before the holidays many years ago.

"Oh, that's Marie next door, she's making her Lebanese cookies," she said.

"Well, what the hell is all that banging," I asked. Fred was wondering too.

"I don't know. I know they're in a mold, maybe that's it," she answered.

"Time to go see," I said.

So we went next door and rang the bell.

Bang! Bang!

What the hell? I thought.

Marie answered the door, traces of flour and Christmas all over her!

"Meme, what the heck are you doing?" we asked.

"Oh," she said exasperated, "I'm making my 'mamoouls,' and they are so hard to get out of the mold."

These are a type of Lebanese filled cookie that is formed in a handmade wooden mold. You press the first piece of dough into the mold, add the filling, and place a piece of dough on top. Press all the edges around and then knock them out, bake, dust with powdered sugar, and eat!

The filling is either pistachio or walnuts, and it's actually very good. Quite a substantial cookie too!

"Every year I go through this, and it takes me forever to get the cookie out. The dough sticks to the mold, and it's hard for them to come out clean," she said, again . . . exasperated!

"Marie," said Fred, "did you ever think of dusting the mold with flour before you put the dough in?"

"Hmmm . . . no, not really," she said.

"Give it a try," he said.

So she dusted the mold, put in the dough, filled, added the top, and . . . you guessed it, one tap and out it came!

"Fred, you saved the day!" She was elated!

"All these years, and all I needed was a bit of flour!"

Marie passed away in 1994, and I was lucky enough to inherit all of her handmade molds. I did make them once, but it seems like without her, they're not the same!

We enjoyed a good laugh, a good cup of coffee, and of course, a great cookie!

God bless you, my dear, you will always live on in my heart!

32

Christmas Eve

"The Plan"

T 'WAS THE night before Christmas.

Yes, it was—a very nice night, clear, cold, and brisk.

I was heading down to spend the evening with Mom, Richard, Michael, Alex, and Samantha. First stop, Susan, wishing all a Merry Christmas!

On December 23rd, we were happy to hear and see that a new baby girl arrived just in time for Christmas! Mary Bailey Giberson, daughter of Eric and Erin, entered this world; and we are certainly happy to see her! Her proud little brother, Garrett, is as excited as can be!

So that's what makes Christmas so wonderful, a season of miracles, visions, dreams, and the time to reflect on how and why we are here. Why are we placed on this earth? What does God have planned for us? For each individual?

Each one of us is part of a plan, a plan we will never know ahead of time, a plan that we must live and wait to see how it works out, or if it doesn't . . . hmm.

I wonder sometimes about the plan. I wonder how it will all fall into place. It will. I have been assured through the years by everyone and by my beliefs, but sometimes you wonder . . . maybe I'm not in the plan. Yes, you are.

We spent Christmas Eve with Mom—me, Michael, Richard, Samantha, and Alex. We always try to make it seem special. It's very difficult to do that sometimes. It's quite different than it used to be. But we all try to make it work. You bring some food that you know she will like, add a tablecloth to the bed tray so it looks different, use plates and silverware and red napkins. Last year, I even brought candles but thought that might be a bad idea. Lots of oxygen going on in that place, wouldn't want the whole place to end up on the moon!

So we do what we can. We talk, we laugh, we think . . . think about the days that have passed, think about the fact that we are now going into the third year in the nursing home. This is actually the third Christmas there. The first one was pretty bad. We didn't stay with her, and it just wasn't good. You felt, well, like shit for leaving.

In the old days, there could have been as many as twenty-four of us all together for Christmas Eve. Yes, it was hectic. Yes, sometimes tense. Yes, sometimes too much drink, too much food, but we were all there. It's tough to make a change like this. It's difficult to go from sitting around a table of many to sitting around a hospital bed of six. It's hard, it's rough, but you do it for Mom. She so enjoyed herself last night.

I didn't have the mental capacity to actually walk around the place last night. In light of what has gone on in the past few months, I decided it wasn't a good idea to look around. I could see some, alone, sad. I couldn't handle it too well. The old lady next to my mom had a visit from her son. She was so happy to see him. They held hands the whole time. It makes me sad but also happy to know that he cared enough to be with her, even for that few moments, long enough to watch Miracle on 34th street, to help her with her dinner, to hold her hand and kiss her good night as he went home to his family. *Whew*, it's hard.

Mom is quiet lately, sometimes just stares, doesn't say anything. She was good last night, not great, but good. My sister visited her today. She didn't talk and hardly opened her eyes. Part of the plan?

She was excited when she heard about the new baby. That was a good thing.

I can't really explain this, but for some reason, I have a very calm sense of things right now. They feel right. They feel like it's going to be okay. Not sure what it is, but I'm going to roll with this right now.

I had a great Christmas this year. I guess knowing that all is well with me, that Mom is well cared for, and that I did have two months at home to recoup made it nice.

I was able to do things for others, make cookies for friends far away, connect with cousins from forty years ago, look for some special things for gifts, and yes, I did hold the true meaning of Christmas close to my heart. But even though I tell you lots of things here, that's something I won't share with you. That's mine.

I don't think we will ever go back to the way things were. How can you? There's an important part missing, but you go build new traditions, new ideas, new thoughts, new experiences. That's life. That's the *plan*! But you never forget the wonderful times that brought you to this point.

Merry Christmas!

33

Happy New Year!

WELL, HERE WE are, 2011, any resolutions out there? Sometimes I wonder why we even bother with these things. Most people don't follow through on them anyway. To me, making resolutions only puts unnecessary pressure on the beginning of what hopes to be a great new year! Maybe it's a good idea just to keep some things rolling around in the back of your head of things you would *like* to accomplish, but not put any pressure on yourself. Start the new year off right—calm, peaceful, full of renewed vigor! Oh boy.

2010 was a good year. A year full of surprises, mystery and some things that just were plain scary! Most of which you have all read about in past chapters.

To some people, moving into a new year is like moving into a new house. Everything has to be boxed up, loaded on a truck, moved to a new location, unpacked, and put away as neatly as possible. You make yourself do this. You make yourself load everything up that happened in the past year. You put it all into one location, then you begin the slow process of unpacking to see exactly which of it you will keep and which to throw out. Sometimes it's a good thing to throw it all out and start all over again!

New Year's Eve is not one of my favorite times. I just can't place my finger on it, but it's just not the greatest night. Although we had a wonderful time this year, as we did last year too. I guess it's more about what is in or on your mind than the actual holiday.

I think about Mom a lot during this time. The funny thing is, she hated that night as well. I can remember when I was home with her that we would go to bed at eleven to miss the midnight crap and wake up the next day in a new year. Never was a big time for us. I hardly ever went to a New Year's Eve party when I was younger, and we've had some pretty quiet ones as the years go on.

But since we discovered the concert at the Kimmel, the last three years have been pretty good. It's just that once we are home, it's usually a quick drink at midnight and then off to bed! It's okay though. It's not a good night to be out and about, and most people are not really interested in coming to a party as they still have to drive home. I wouldn't want to be in that crowd at Times Square, but I would like to spend one New Year's in Las Vegas! Yes, sir, just once!

But my ultimate time would be in Vienna and then attend the New Year's concert there. We watch it every year, and it looks like quite a good time. Of course, you have to enjoy that music and dancing, but that's another "bucket list" item for me!

I hear about different parties and how great they were. "Yes, the party was really great! We got so drunk."

How do you know you had a good time? Makes me wonder. If you have to get drunk to enjoy the party.

So now it's time to think about the New Year ahead. As I said earlier, no resolutions to put any unnecessary pressure on. Just the ideas that will develop in my head and hopefully come to fruition at some point during the year. This way you won't disappoint yourself.

After two months of recuperating, I have to return to work tomorrow. It's a good time to go back, a new year, a new house, so to speak, and new thoughts and ideas.

There is one thing I am going to attempt this year. I am going to go back and see how I can put all these thoughts and words into some type of novel. It may take a few years. I may have to add some things that others may not like, but I want to start, want to try to see what happens.

Happy New Year to all!

I will continue to write my thoughts and hope you will continue to read them!

34

27 years later . . .

1973 WAS THE year that I began my career in retail. Excited, young, fresh, eager to learn new things and get involved with working at something I really love!

Creating new looks, learning about new ideas, conveying that to the consumer so they can understand and buy! That's the name of the game.

Make it look great and the consumer will purchase it!

Thirty-eight years in retail! Thirty-eight years of doing just about anything to make a shop look good, make a department appealing, make the holidays come alive in ways that you wouldn't do at home! How exciting!

Working in a department store can be fun, but it is also extremely exhausting! Long hours, long days, and forget the holidays. They were just more days that you had to work, had to get it all out and up so that the guest could look, *oohh* and *ahhh*, and then buy something!

It was fun though, always had a good team to work with, made new friends, and mostly had no problem with the long hours and the hard work. Fun, most of the time.

In 1986, it was time to get out of the store! Time to expand and see if there was life after the store experience. I was lucky. My store manager from where I was accepted a job at ARA Services, located at the Philly airport. The retail was anyway. At that time, we had about twelve airports to do and many stores within each airport.

My month of November was a simple one, go from airport to airport, all over the country, and install Christmas decorations. It took me almost the entire month to hit every one, but I did it, all alone! The same was true for special promotions, always the same thing, from airport to airport with the occasional stop at some type of sports venue, every once in a while, a national park. This went on for many years.

Because Miami International was such a big place and required extra work, I was able to hire an assistant there. My first one lasted about a year. He was more interested in how many women he could nail at the airport than setting up and maintaining the shops. Oh he could set things up okay, but not the right stuff. I can't really remember how many different ones we went through down there. It was a difficult place, and we finally got out of the airport business. But before we leave Miami, let me tell you this one.

Kevin, a young, energetic individual came to work for us there. He was originally from Boston, a fairly well-placed family. He moved to Miami, started to work with us. He was much the fashion plate! Had something new almost every day. How did he do it? I used to think.

"Well, usually I use my expense checks to buy new clothes. Then I have my mother pay my credit card." Needless to say, that didn't last very long, and she cut him off. At that time, we did not have corporate cards, and we had to use our own card for hotels, meals, and if allowed, rental car. It was tough. We didn't always get reimbursed quickly.

He continued to work for us and established a relationship with one of the girls that worked there too. She was the general manager there, and he kind of worked for her, and I supervised him from afar. They got along okay, in the beginning. But she was a bit controlling and always tested their relationship. Basically, she was a bitch!

They lasted for a while. I listened to him complain about her and she, about him. But we needed someone on-site, and he really did do some great work.

So picture this. There's a new terminal shop being set up. It's late. Everyone is tired, working on this for weeks. In comes Kevin. He was working in a different airport that day; sometimes he did if he was needed. She was pissed, let him have it, in front of the entire group. (Mind you, I wasn't there, but had expert eye witnesses!)

He had had enough.

"May I have your attention please?" he screamed to the group.

"Mary Lou is a lesbian and a drunk!" he cried out.

Well, that ended his career for us. "Get your things and leave the terminal immediately!" his manager said. So no more Kevin, no more Marylou, no more Miami. Thank God!

Another one bites the dust.

One of our managers in Boise, Idaho, had a friend that was interested in the job. He was willing to move to Philly so we could actually keep an eye on him, and we would travel together to do the projects. He lasted about a year or so, too much traveling and his personality didn't fit. He didn't have the best talent for the job, and he succeeded in other things after he left.

I was getting tired of traveling. I didn't know if I could do it anymore. Our boss at the time was a dick! He hated being home with his wife and rotten kids, so he traveled all the time. Problem was, he always wanted someone to go with him. And he was notorious for not telling you until the day before. I just couldn't do it anymore, so I spoke to the HR man, no help there, and I quit. Not a good move as far as Fred was concerned. But I couldn't do it.

I went to work for a sign company as a rep. Not good for me, I don't take rejection well. I wasn't pushy enough, and in the long run, I ended up losing money!

I then went to work for a local fixture company. That was better. I did do sales, but not cold-calling and that worked out well, for a year or so anyway, then the crotchety old owner decided that I was taking business away from her doing freelance on the side, and off I went. The only great thing about working there was my friend Sylvia! Still doing business and a good friend to this day!

Yikes! Now what?

Well, as luck would have it, my replacement at ARA didn't work out; and I was asked to come back to do freelance work. I did so for about six months and then asked why they didn't hire me full-time?

They did, and yes, the old boss was there. But I needed the work. They said that I would be back full-time at the start of the new fiscal year. Just weeks away! Great! I think.

Well, I started back in October, and within a few weeks the boss was fired! Yes! This was a good sign. Here we go.

That was almost twenty-seven years ago, and here I am.

We don't have any airports anymore, mostly National Parks, some special accounts and stadiums and arenas. Oh, they're ball parks now. We have many.

Things got better, the work was hard, but it was planned out. The travel was planned, so you knew when and where you were going.

I love it, always did though.

I take pride in my work, do the best I can. Spend many hours and days on projects, miss lots of family life that I am truly sorry for now.

But I wanted to do the best job. I wanted people to know that they could count on me and that I was going to give them the best I could whenever they needed it! Isn't that the right way to do it? Isn't that part of the values that you were taught growing up? Isn't that what gives you the feeling of satisfaction at night when you lay your head to rest? You'd think that, wouldn't you?

You establish relationships throughout the country. People know what you can do and know that you will always make it work for them. You give it your all!

So here's the purpose of this story.

After almost twenty-seven years of doing what I do, and doing it well, making millions for the company, someone comes along and decides that things are going to change. We're going to divide the business in two—one Sports and one Parks. I took care of both. Now I have one, Sports. Such a big fan I am!

The thing is, I worked so hard in the Parks for all these years. I made contacts and learned all about what goes on in each and every location. I took pride in making things look great and helping to promote the beauty that lies within each one, and one individual can make it all go away. Pretty sad, and yes, I am having a hard time, but as they say, "At least you have a job!" Hmmm, I know my Annette will do a good job even though we won't be working together.

35

Maybe it's not the end . . .

"WE'RE ORPHANS!" CRIED our good friend Reggie as she hugged me as I entered my sister's house.

Orphans, I often thought of that as a kid. My mom once told me that if anything should happen to her or my father that we would have to go and live with my grandparents. Now where do we go? They're all gone!

I wasn't sure what to call this chapter. I'm not sure if it is really the *end*, or is it the beginning? Is it the start of a new direction in life? I definitely know it is the end of a major era!

My mother has passed, after two and a half years in the nursing home, countless times that she said that this was her last day, hour, or minute. God took her home on the early evening of March 26, took her to a place that would unite her with Dad and all the loved ones that have left before her.

She was the last of the incredible women of First Avenue that included Reggie's parents, the last of the girlfriends from a block that became a part of all of us. One we left many years ago, but one that was constantly on her mind.

"I went to the house today!" she would tell us.

"Why is the door unlocked, and there is food in the refrigerator?" she said. "I thought I sold it, but I went there today."

This went on for several weeks before her death, and I think she was slowly going to a place that she really wanted to be. She remembered that house as being the best years of her life. All was well there. Dad was not a stroke patient. We all were born there, and there was peace and happiness. Well, most of time, maybe not the time she got really mad at something and threw all the dishes on the floor!

"Easy, Elizabeth," my dad would say calmly. Then he would clean up the mess.

I can guarantee you that if my siblings read this, they will say, "There goes Peter again in his rose-colored glasses!" Maybe so, but I'll always wear them!

It's taken me a while to be able to write this. I have so many thoughts and emotions to deal with that I couldn't get it together.

"Every day will get better," everyone says. "I know it will, just takes a bit of time. My fear is that it will go too quickly. Memories will fade. People will be forgotten. I don't want that to happen. I won't let it."

There were times that weren't the best. There were struggles, and there were differences. We all have them. But we go on. We do what we have to, and we make the best of every situation.

We become strong. We build character, and we build our independence, our being.

The hardest thing in the world was seeing her in the state that she was in, even harder for my sister who couldn't understand why she didn't want to push herself, why she didn't want to walk, get out of bed, get out of the chair, and gain back her independence.

Did we baby her? Sure did. All of us. But I will speak for myself here.

At forty years old, her life came to a screeching halt! The man she loved was now taken down by stroke! There were five of us, all at home. The youngest was about five. Now what? Well, we did okay, but I know there are many stories that happened that I don't know about. Little by little, I am finding out that things weren't always the best. But we did stay together.

As I told her younger sister on the phone last week, "We are here to comfort each other." That's what we do. We all have a different way to mourn and different feelings, but we all need the same thing. The same compassion and understanding to help get through this tough time.

I think of her every day. I thank God that when I did visit her, she would ask me to hold her hand. Now, if I place one hand in the other, I feel the warmth of hers. I feel that hand that I held. It makes me cry now. One day it will make me happy.

I am grateful that she no longer has to sit and wonder about tomorrow, wonder what will happen and where she will go. All she wanted to do was go home. Go home and be with her Whitey. That's all that mattered in the last weeks.

Funny thing is, I knew it was coming. Just didn't know when, but could tell by the way she looked and by what I felt. I knew it wasn't going to be a long time for her, and I knew that she would then be free. I only wish I knew if she were happy now. They all tell me she is. I think she is too.

God does have a plan. I know that. He didn't want any of us there to see her, and he took her so quickly. That was a blessing, for her, for us.

Everything was planned in advance.

"I want to wear the red dress and coat that Fred gave me, my pearls, and I would like a pair of gold slippers." She would tell us this so often. My sister had her dress cleaned and ready from the time we left her apartment. The only thing was to buy the gold slippers. I hope she doesn't mind that we bought them in Target!

I know people say how nice someone looks in the coffin. But I have to tell you . . . she did. She looked like she did many years before all this happened. She really did look peaceful and had a gentle, sweet smile on her face. It really was a comfort to see that.

"No viewing," she told us. "Just you kids come and see me and then we'll go to church." We honored that as best we could by allowing her sisters, brother, and a few relatives pay their respects.

I wanted it to be beautiful, peaceful. I wanted a wonderful tribute to her. I also wanted everything to match, to coordinate, and be gorgeous. Music, flowers, the whole thing.

And it was, a full, packed church, a grand tribute to her and her family.

I was asked to do a reading, me and my nephew, her first grandson. I asked her for strength and the ability to do this without breaking down. I did it. For her, I did it. She gave me the strength.

As we walked down the aisle at the end of the service, the soloist was singing "Let There Be Peace on Earth." She sang it so beautifully that I could feel the angels soaring above, and I could sense that she was happy, happy to be home, happy to be with her Whitey, all her family and friends.

At that moment, it was such a powerful feeling for me—a calming, wonderful feeling that I hold on to every day!

My two younger brothers spent almost every day with her the last two-plus years, at least once a day, sometimes more. Michael cared for her with Maryann like she was his child. Richard brought her special food and drinks, and the rest of us tried to get there as often as possible.

Sometimes Fred would visit with me, and they would always have a good laugh. She did laugh. She laughed a lot.

Well, I don't know if I want this to be the end. I don't know if I want to stop writing. We'll see.

I miss her every day . . . every day.

36

Significance of it all . . .

LAST NIGHT WE watched a movie titled *The Cry of the Owl*. Kind of dark, not the happiest of movies, but it did shed a light.

On the day my mom died, this is what happened prior to the call.

I was returning from the store around 5:00 p.m. (The call came in around 8:00 p.m.) It was still light out. Thanks to daylight savings time, and the weather was clear, maybe a little windy.

I turned onto my street, and as I approached the beginning of my property line, I could see this enormous black turkey buzzard! His (or her) wings were fully extended. They looked to be about six feet wide. I never saw such a bird in the area. Although I've been told since then that they are all around and are capable of picking up a small animal! Watch out, Herman and Heidi! Well, maybe they're too fat!

Anyway, I slowed down, approached the area, and watched. He closed his wings and flew into the tree. As I glanced up, in the tree sitting on the branch was this incredibly beautiful blonde-colored owl. He was very majestic and very beautiful! I, once again, never in all the sixteen years living here saw such a creature.

I stopped the car, looked up at him, and I could see his head turn to look at me! Why! Maybe he was afraid of the car.

I went in the garage, parked the car, and went to get Fred.

"Come out and look at these birds. I think it's an owl in the tree!' I said.

We came out, and all that was there was the black bird. The owl was gone.

So last night, as I watched this movie, they stated in it that the owl was a messenger of death. Hmmm, I was convinced then and now totally that I was given a sign.

How do we know these signals? How do we know if they have meaning before the happening? How do we read this and see where it will take us?

The answer, in my mind, is we never will. We'll never know because we try not to think about the possibility that there is some force that is creating and controlling these feelings. We are taught, at least in my religion and upbringing, that you do not question the will of God! You do not ask why.

And I try and try every day not to ask, and not to ask about my mom. I know she was eighty-four, and she basically had an okay life. We did everything we could for her. I'm not questioning that, but I miss her so much every day, and I hope and pray that she is holding my dad's hand as I write this and having a peaceful rest.

The things that I question are, why would a mother drive her car into the water and kill her children? Why is there a monster in command in countries that don't even have food to eat and they worship him?

I can't even question why my dad became ill at fifty-three and had to be cared for every day. I can't, because I know he didn't take his medicine and his blood pressure created this issue.

I know we all have questions, all have beliefs that we were taught at an early age and some we learned just from living life.

Don't look for the signs, don't look for the answers, just look ahead, and when you hit that occasional speed bump, just slow down, regroup, and continue on your life's path!

Peace.

37

Epilogue

LIFE CHANGES, AS I have said earlier, with the blink of an eye!

After spending all of my years centering my life around Mom, I find it strange and sometimes sad that she is gone. I talk to her daily, not a crazy thing, just a need. Nothing wrong with that as long as you keep it in perspective.

I know that it has been difficult for me to drive to Asbury Park knowing that she is not there. I haven't done it yet, not sure when I will, and I only hope that my family understands.

I have so many more things to write about, so look for the next book in the future!

I sure hope you enjoyed this, and I want to thank everyone that has touched my life, those that are here and those that are gone.

CPSIA information can be obtained at www.ICGtesting.com
Printed in the USA
BVOW021706290312

286406BV00001B/103/P